Wild Pony Whispering

The real life story of how an orphaned Exmoor pony foal
helped us to tame and understand the wild ponies of Exmoor

DAWN WESTCOTT

HALSGROVE

First published in Great Britain in 2015
Copyright © Dawn Westcott 2015
© The photographers in respect of their individual contributions

British Library Cataloguing-in-Publication Data
A CIP record for this title is available from the British Library

ISBN 978 0 85704 276 7

HALSGROVE

Halsgrove House, Ryelands Business Park,
Bagley Road, Wellington, Somerset TA21 9PZ
Tel: 01823 653777   Fax: 01823 216796
email: sales@halsgrove.com

Part of the Halsgrove group of companies
Information on all Halsgrove titles is
 available at: www.halsgrove.com

Printed in China by
Everbest Printing Co Ltd

Contents

This book is dedicated to:

My husband Nick Westcott without whom none of this would have been possible. After a lifetime's involvement with horses, Nick rediscovered Exmoor ponies when we married in 2008 and has since fully embraced the breed and generously given over much of his farm to allow not just the creation of Holtball Exmoor Pony Stud but also the Exmoor Pony Club and Moorland Exmoor Foal Project. Without his support and help, I could not have trained our Exmoor stallion, Hawkwell Versuvius 'Bear' to win two world championships in International Horse Agility, to save Monsieur Chapeau and the other moorland foals, and to campaign for an end to harmful practices like multiple hot branding (applying an excessive number of brands to foals). His courage, expertise and resilience have helped to bring together some of Exmoor's most progressive moorland farmers and landowners to form the Moorland Exmoor Pony Breeders Group and we have seen immense improvement in Exmoor pony moorland breeding practices, management, promotion and opportunities in a short time. There is still much work to be done and I would like to thank Nick Westcott from the bottom of my heart for his absolute support, encouragement, friendship and love – for his family, the ponies and Exmoor itself. Without him, this book would not have been written.

Acknowledgements and Thanks

Dawn would also like to thank the following organisations and people for their help, support and encouragement:

My mother Heather Williams for her unwavering support, encouragement and belief. Our very special friends, volunteers and supporters: Judy Bethell, June Eckhart, Sue Byrne, Kate South, Kate Hele, Maya Horsey, Monty Roberts and his family, Christina Willoughby-White, Josephine Laing, Melanie Maddocks, Carol Jackson, Gareth Latham, Peter Hotchkiss, Alyson Govier and Tony Andrews, Miriam Main, John Main, Susan Richardson, Julie Cope, Susan French, Leslie Nichols, Bette Baldwin, Brenda Lamb, Margaret Quinn Evans, Jim Evans, Amelia Phillips, Jasmine Adams, Elaine Tomlinson, Sian Thomas, Helen Disberry, Helen Spinks, Joyce Mrozielski, Maureen Harvey, Helen Disberry, Simon and Tracey David and all the others that I haven't managed to mention.

Thanks also to our fellow Exmoor moorland farmers and friends and their passion and commitment for their pony herds: Nigel and Maria Floyd and family, Rex and Banger Milton & family, Robin Milton, William Dart and family, Mr & Mrs South, Christine Allen, Ian and Helen South, Kate South, James Bryant and Roz Leworthy, Matthew Coldicutt, Ben and Christina Williams, the Wyatt family and Dr Lisa Wojan (USA).

To the dedicated team at Exmoor National Park Authority – especially Sarah Bryan and Nigel Stone. A special mention for vet Peter Green BVSc Cert EO MRCVS who has highlighted many of the issues concerning the Exmoor pony breed in his report "The Free-Living Ponies of Exmoor National Park – Their Status, Welfare & Future" and who continues to work for the good of the ponies. And to Western Counties Equine Hospital, Clive Ponsford and Andrea Hicks.

Photographers: Gareth Latham, Lisa & Jamie Waters, Dawn Westcott, Tricia Gibson, Nick Westcott, June Eckhart, Judy Bethell, Kate South, Kate Hele, Julia Proctor, Tracey David, Amelia Phillips, Clive Ponsford, Mike Mellor and Valerie Powell

Organisations: Exmoor National Park Authority and the National Trust Holnicote Estate.

Find out more about

The Exmoor Pony Club,
The Moorland Exmoor Foal Project,
Holtball Exmoor Pony Stud
(Herd 11), The Moorland Exmoor
Pony Breeders Group (MEPBG)
at www.Exmoor Pony Club.co.uk.
Twitter @ExmoorPonyClub
www.facebook.com/ExmoorPonyClub
Holtball Exmoor Pony Stud, Holt Ball
Farm, Luccombe, Minehead, Somerset
TA24 8SZ. Tel 01643 862466
email exmoorponyclub@hotmail.co.uk

Introduction

This is the real-life story of Monsieur Chapeau, a wild, orphaned Exmoor pony foal found severely malnourished with pneumonia on the moors of Exmoor and how he survived and thrived beyond all expectations – bringing with him the secrets of how to create a bond of trust and friendship with the wild Exmoor ponies.

The subsequent struggle to get Monsieur Chapeau recognised and registered as a true Moorland Exmoor highlights the plight of the free-living ponies of Exmoor National Park that threatens their very existence. This book follows Monsieur Chapeau and other foals like him and the quest to safeguard the future of this endangered ancient native breed. Horse whispering becomes pony whispering as a wild Exmoor pony connects with man to secure his survival – with the character, wisdom and generosity of heart to inspire better understanding of the equine mind. This story will appeal to those with a love of Exmoor and its flora and fauna and also provides an invaluable practical guide for people interested in 'connecting' with horses through trust-based liberty handling and socialisation – from the perspective of the enigmatic Exmoor ponies.

Nick and Dawn Westcott already run the Moorland Exmoor Foal Project and Dawn is twice International Horse Agility world champion with their moorbred stallion Hawkwell Versuvius 'Bear', who is ridden as well as standing at stud at Holt Ball. Now Monsieur Chapeau reaches out from the moor and shows Dawn that there is more that must be done to ensure the successful preservation of the wild Exmoor ponies – and improve their welfare, wellbeing and opportunities – and the way they are handled and trained.

Opposite: Dawn Westcott
with Monsieur Chapeau

Chapter 1
The Free-living Ponies of Exmoor

Exmoor National Park is home to the captivating and characterful ancient breed of British Native Hill Pony called the 'Exmoor'.

These mostly free-living semi-feral ponies have grazed the wilds of the moor for hundreds if not thousands of years and are very much part of the flora and fauna. This spectacularly beautiful moorland and coastal area nestles in the exquisite corner of South West England that stretches from North Devon across into West Somerset and is adjacent to the Bristol Channel with views across to Wales. Much of the area was originally known as The Royal Hunting Forest and was the last place in England to have tarmac roads. The 267.5 square miles of steep and challenging terrain of moorland, combes, forests and cliffs made navigating Exmoor difficult, so it remained relatively isolated and retained its breathtaking natural beauty.

In the early 1920s, a group of Exmoor farmers decided to select some of the free-living ponies running on the moorland area that was, in 1954, to become Exmoor National Park, and establish a pedigree 'Exmoor Pony breed'. They formed the Exmoor Pony Society in 1921 and the records show that various brown, black, grey, bay and dun ponies were present on the moors when the original selections were made. Over time, the 'breed standard' was created and the ponies were 'bred to type'. And so the Exmoor pony evolved into the ponies you see grazing the moors today and they bear striking similarity to the equines depicted in ancient artworks. No white markings are allowed and the ponies have to conform to a strict set of physical characteristics which are assessed during an inspection as foals, before they can be registered as pedigree Exmoor ponies.

Each autumn, the herds are gathered in from the various moorland enclosures and driven to their respective farms where the farmers put them forward for inspection and registration. In the early 2000s, it became a registration requirement that both the sire and dam of each moorbred (free-living) Exmoor foal had to be confirmed through DNA testing. Until 2014, Exmoor pony foals that

Opposite: The Tippbarlake Herd 387 ponies being gathered from Brendon Common

passed inspection were also hot branded with up to seven large marks, including the Exmoor Pony 'Star', their herd number and their individual pony number, on their shoulder and rump. This required the foals to be forcibly restrained, often at the same time as being removed from their familiar free-living environment and weaned from their mothers. As a result of this understandable trauma, and being naturally 'wild' in nature, many Exmoor ponies subsequently found it difficult to trust humans and gained a reputation for being rather 'difficult' to handle. Much work has been carried out to improve the ponies' welfare and in 2014 DEFRA introduced a

Farleywater Dazzler with her dam living wild and free with H67 herd on Buscombe

Code of Practice for the Identification of Semi-Feral Ponies which restricted the number of hot brands that can be applied, and to semi-feral foals returning to the moors only. Work continues to bring an end to this painful and stressful practice completely.

Exmoor ponies currently feature on the Rare Breeds Survival Trust Category Two 'Endangered Breeds' list (300-500 breeding mares worldwide). Their numbers dropped to around 50 ponies and six stallions after the Second World War, which nearly rendered the breed extinct and over the years, their numbers have gradually been bred up again to around 3,000 - 4,000 worldwide. The 500 or so free-living ponies of Exmoor National Park are particularly important because living and breeding here, in their indigenous, natural environment, within their family herds, enables the ponies to retain their unique characteristics and behaviours – and the 'True Moorland Type'.

Exmoor ponies have survived and thrived in the challenging and varied Exmoor terrain, with its harsh weather conditions, which more domesticated horse and pony breeds would not be able to tolerate. Through evolving in this wilderness, where some of the moorland enclosures span thousands of acres, the Exmoor pony is strong, robust, highly intelligent, independent thinking and self-sufficient. They grow immensely thick double-layered winter coats, substantial manes and tails and have a variety of useful features to help them withstand relentless periods of wind, rain and cold weather, with little to eat and sometimes sparse shelter. The protective padding around what is described as their 'toad' eyes is designed to dispel rain; their substantial jaws and teeth enable them to munch through large quantities of coarse vegetation; their barrel-chested, rotund bodies can cope with digesting rough moorland grasses, gorse, and small branches and foliage; and their short, strong legs with tough black feet enable them to traverse the varied terrain and remain sound. Their distinctive 'mealy' (pale) markings and wonderful range of gold, red, brown, bay and black colouring helps them to stay camouflaged in their moorland environment, as well as giving them their beautiful appearance.

One of the moorland areas – the approximately 5,500 acres of Dunkery and Nutscale Commons – stretches up from the Porlock Vale to Dunkery Beacon and over to Nutscale Reservoir and Alderman's Barrow, running back across Ley Hill, Cloutsham Ball, Webber's Post, Horner Woods and the Horner River Valley. This challenging moorland terrain provides a wonderful yet harsh environment for the free-living Exmoor ponies and it really can be a case of 'survival of the fittest'. It was here, in this magnificent National Park, that a little, free-living colt foal had become separated from his mother and herd and was all alone, severely malnourished and beginning to lose his battle to survive, in a steep wooded combe high up on Dunkery.

Chapter 2
The Rescue of Monsieur Chapeau

In the middle of a cold, wet and harsh January, a tiny, starving late-born Exmoor pony foal was spotted by a walker in the steep combe running down to Cloutsham Watersplash, which nestles under Dunkery Beacon – the highest point in Exmoor National Park at 1700ft.

The little colt foal had been separated from his mother and herd for some time and he was all alone and in a weakened state. That day, he'd climbed up through an undergrowth of moss-covered, knarled tree roots and a slippery carpet of sodden fallen leaves onto the path which walker Tricia was navigating, and stared beseechingly at her. She was moved by his plight and that evening alerted nearby moorland farmers, Nick and Dawn Westcott, who run the Moorland Exmoor Foal Project. Early the following morning they went out to find the foal and assess the situation. Dawn Westcott tells the story of Moorland Exmoor pony, Monsieur Chapeau:

Early that morning, the rain was lashing at the windscreen as we made our way up from the National Trust Holnicote Estate village of Luccombe to the car park at Webber's Post to meet Tricia and her husband Peter. We unloaded the quad bike from the horse trailer and traversed the moor on the bike and on foot to try and locate the orphaned foal – while the heavy, freezing downpour continued unabated. We eventually spotted him half way down the steep combe where he was standing forlorn amongst the trees and trying to nibble at the fallen leaves, moss and other sparse vegetation. He made a pitiful sight, obviously severely malnourished and unsteady on his legs, and it was clear that he needed some immediate help. The challenge was working out how to approach him, catch him and then persuade him to come with us so we could get him to safety. The foal may have fared better in crisp, cold weather, but we'd recently been subjected to one of the wettest winters in years – and prolonged, relentless rain is trying for any free-living animal. As a result, he was drenched and shivering and couldn't even summon the energy to trot away from us.

Climbing onto the path where he was spotted by a walker

Opposite: A plea for help, staring beseechingly at the walker

Opposite, clockwise from top left: So weak he needed frequent rests on the way out of the combe; willing to make contact; making our way down the path to the road; loading into the trailer

Below: severely malnourished with a swollen belly

The combe was steep as well as slippery, so we had to make our way down carefully, zig-zagging so as not to drive the foal away, and also taking care not to lose our footing. Tricia, Peter and myself made our way downwards, while Nick took the bike to the bottom of the combe and started walking up towards the foal. We approached very carefully and paused frequently to try to convey to him that we weren't going to 'attack'. The biggest fear of these wild ponies – or indeed any wild animal – is being caught and restrained as they think they're going to die. In the event, it didn't take too much effort to surround the foal and put a head collar on him and the poor little chap sank to the ground. He was so tired and weak that he accepted our help very quickly, probably realising that we were the best chance he'd got. We did wonder if he'd be able to make it down the hillside to the road where we could transport him to safety. His eyes were sunken and hollow and the vertebrae along his spine were raised and exposed – he was basically

nothing but skin and bones under his thick, matted coat and his starving little belly was worryingly distended. But it was his wheezing that caused most concern and we could see that he was close to not making it at all. The chill had got to his lungs and he was displaying alarming signs of pneumonia.

Although understandably wary at the close proximity of humans, the foal seemed to understand that we were trying to help him and he was surprisingly calm and quickly got the idea of how to walk along on the lead ropes. His little legs were struggling to carry him though and he frequently collapsed, at which time we'd sit quietly stroking him until he could summon the strength to carry on. It was during these pauses that I realised this was a very special little pony who despite his obvious predicament, could still find the curiosity to respond with warmth to being stroked, and would gently 'sniff noses'. Eventually, we managed to navigate the combe, crossed the stream and finally made our way down to the road. The foal waited quietly with the others while I jogged back up to Webber's Post and drove the trailer back down to meet them. He loaded without protest and we made the short journey back to the farm at Holt Ball. He walked calmly down the ramp into his new accommodations and stood there, drenched, shivering and wheezing. Some of the other foals in the Moorland Exmoor Foal Project came in to peer at him through the gate and he studied them solemnly. Then he gently reached forwards and sniffed our noses, as if to say thank you, which as you can imagine was very moving. So here he was, safely at Holt Ball, and finally out of the driving rain and wind. Already this little scrap of a pony had touched all of our hearts with his courage, calmness and cooperation – and the trust he had placed in us as his rescuers. Now it was a question of seeing if we had found him in time and could nurse him back to health. Fortunately, he showed immediate interest in the little pile of haylage I'd placed beside him which was a promising sign.

The vet confirmed that the foal did indeed have pneumonia and warned us that it would be 'touch and go' for him over the next few days and not to be surprised if he just 'slipped away'. He prescribed a course of various antibiotics, injections and drenches and the treatment began. However, as soon as a feed bowl was presented, he tucked in immediately and didn't surface until it was all gone. We had to take care to feed him small, regular meals to allow his poor, swollen belly to cope with the reintroduction of food. However, Nick remarked that as long as he continued to show such an interest in his feeds, he had a very good chance of making it. The foal also accepted having his head collar on and off and took the drenches without protest, and this made it much easier to ensure that he had the right treatment at the right time. It was certainly a relief that, from day one, he appeared to have the appetite of a lion and looked determined to try and survive.

Top: Giving comfort when he needed to rest
Above: Waiting to go into the trailer

Opposite, clockwise from top: Sniffing noses and conveying reassurance that all will be well; meeting the other Moorland Exmoor Foal Project youngsters through the gate; Monsieur Chapeau again offers this special nose-to-nose gesture on arrival at Holt Ball

How did Monsieur Chapeau get his Name?

Soon after mentioning his rescue on our Exmoor Pony Club and Moorland Exmoor Foal Project social media, our friend in France, Carol, wrote 'Chapeau to the rescue team!'

When we asked her what it meant she said, 'In France, it means "I take my hat off to you!"'

Well of course, we took our hats off to the brave little orphaned foal for surviving against the odds and showing such courage when rescued – so he was bestowed the grand name of 'Monsieur Chapeau'!

After contacting the owners of the two Exmoor pony herds running out on the Dunkery Commons, both agreed that whichever herd it turned out that Monsieur Chapeau was from, we should take over his ownership. He was now officially a Holtball Exmoor pony.

Monsieur Chapeau's Early Rehabilitation

Monsieur Chapeau continued to accept the drenches and medication, which included aloe vera liquid and probiotics. His coat was in a dreadful state and when it eventually dried out, it became apparent that he had various rainscald areas (where scabs form on the skin around the hair follicles and can cause sore and bare areas), a mass of dreadlocks and goodness knows what else all knotted up in there. I spent hours with Monsieur Chapeau, gradually working through his matted coat, and often he was happy to remain lying down while I gently brushed and combed him. Sometimes he'd get sleepy and lie down flat across my lap for a snooze. When he wasn't snoozing, he munched his way through his meals and haylage with great enthusiasm. Not once did he attempt to bite, kick or make any untoward gesture. We had established a bond of trust that first day, and Monsieur Chapeau was comfortable with the status quo. He thankfully made it through those first few days and fortunately the antibiotics worked and he started recovering from the pneumonia. However, he remained rather weak and needed help to stand up for the first ten days, but each day brought improvement. You could not have wished for a better patient – his will to live was incredible. And so was his appetite!

Opposite, top left to right: Monsieur Chapeau needed help standing up for the first ten days; accepting his drenches and medication; comfort and reassurance

Centre left to right: Tucking into his food; trusting us from the first day; working on the tangles in his coat

Bottom left to right: More cuddles; accepting his head collar on and off; starting to look more sprightly

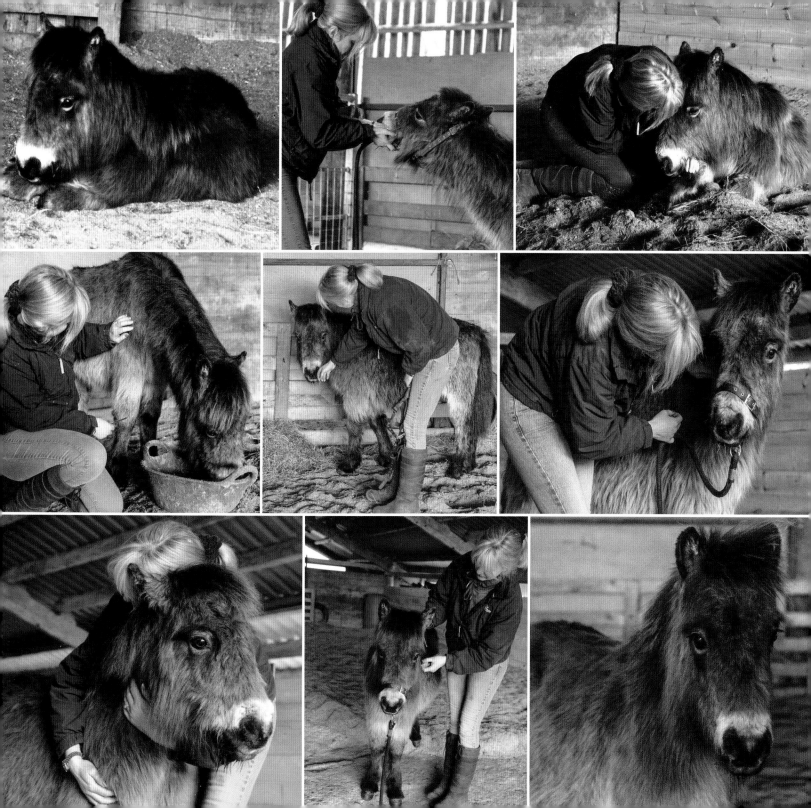

Monsieur Chapeau and Farleywater Lady Stumpkin Pumpkin

Greeting the other foals through the gate in his barn area was a highlight for Monsieur Chapeau and whenever they came in, they showed great interest in him. He had the radio on at times during the day and there was plenty of farm activity to be viewed from his barn accommodations which gave him the use of an area about 45ft x 15ft. However, there was nothing quite like some fellow equine company and he thoroughly enjoyed sniffing noses with the other foals. One of the filly foals, Farleywater Lady Stumpkin Pumpkin, started spending a lot of time at the gate and made it very clear that she wanted to come into Monsieur Chapeau's enclosure. She had perhaps noticed that he was given a couple more meals each day than the other foals and the accommodations looked decidedly spacious. There were obviously 'special privileges' to be had in Monsieur Chapeau's area and Lady Stumpkin Pumpkin was determined to get in there. Watching Pumpkin work all this out and convey her desire to join Monsieur Chapeau was fascinating. So one day, when Monsieur Chapeau had regained enough strength to stand up on his own, we let her in to see how they got on. As Pumpkin was so much bigger than Monsieur Chapeau, and also very keen on her food, we wondered if she would prevent him from getting his due portions. We

Monsieur Chapeau guards his feed bowl

Monsieur Chapeau and Pumpkin are soon good friends

Pumpkin often lay close to Monsieur Chapeau

needn't have worried. Nothing was going to keep MC from his feed bowl and he expressed that view with gusto to Pumpkin, who was rather taken aback. While he may have been weak after his ordeal, his mighty spirit was most certainly fully intact.

They got on really well, so Pumpkin started spending a few hours with Monsieur Chapeau each day. Soon she would come in with the other foals in the evening and go straight to the gate to be let in with him where they remained until the following morning. She seemed determined to take him under her wing and was both bustling and bossy and also affectionate with him. MC seemed to look forward to her visits – however, in those early days he also required a lie down and a sleep after she'd gone back out to join the herd.

There was no doubt that their friendship accelerated his recovery. In turn, Pumpkin's own socialisation and handling progressed rapidly as she responded to the trust he offered us. She watched intently as he let me groom him and sit with him and she became more comfortable and curious about interacting with me. I was able to stroke her and brush her too and as she was free to stay there or walk away, her trust and confidence increased and she became bolder. Monsieur Chapeau loved his coat being brushed while he was lying down and Pumpkin started lying down next to us. It wasn't long before Pumpkin let me groom her while she was lying down too, which was a considerable advancement in her socialisation. And it was no surprise that soon after extending this trust, she willingly allowed me to put a head collar on her.

Left: Farleywater Lady Stumpkin Pumpkin interacting with the feather duster

Below left: Pumpkin letting Dawn brush her tail

Below right: Pumpkin allowing Dawn to put on her head collar

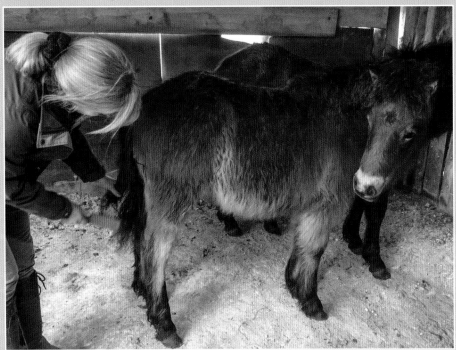

Monsieur Chapeau's calm presence in the barn had started to contribute significantly to the socialisation work with the other foals. You could literally feel his positive vibes and he radiated a soothing reassurance. Already, his behaviour had extended the parameters of learning for us regarding the sentient capabilities of the ponies, who had all been born wild and free on the moor. Each day, Monsieur Chapeau grew a little stronger and started to gain condition. The wheezing had disappeared and, thankfully, he was beginning to properly recover. He had certainly won Lady Stumpkin Pumpkin's heart – she clearly adored him.

A wonderful bond developed between Monsieur Chapeau and Farleywater Lady Stumpkin Pumpkin

Lady Stumpkin Pumpkin in the Learning Zone with Dawn Westcott

Monsieur Chapeau Goes Out in the Pasture!

During Monsieur Chapeau's early rehabilitation, although he loved Lady Stumpkin Pumpkin's company, he also needed 'quiet time' to continue his recovery and build his strength, and made no protest when she went out in the mornings. However, after a couple of weeks, as soon as Pumpkin left one morning, he began leaping and bucking around his enclosure. As it was a fairly large area, he could pick up quite a speed and it was heartening to see him able to engage such energy – he was telling us in no uncertain terms that it was time for him to join the others in the pasture too. While his body was not quite as ready as his mind for turnout with a herd of boisterous foals, we felt a little time in the pasture was just what he needed after his barn rest and would do his spirit the world of good. Pumpkin had sensed his frustration and came back into the barn again, as if to collect him. After separating the two larger colts for this first session, we decided to let Monsieur Chapeau out for a little exploration. It was quite something to watch – he was rather cautious at first, walking calmly out of the barn into the corral and surveying the pasture from the gate. He walked down into the field and stared across to the other foals, pausing there. Then he gave a feisty springing leap and flew across to them like a little stallion, kicking his heels with tail lifted high – full of presence and his shaggy coat streaming in the wind. The fillies were fairly robust with him at first, but Lady Stumpkin Pumpkin was around and about to look after him. It was wonderful to see this tiny little scrap of a pony, with his woolly mammoth coat, pulling himself up to his full height and trotting and cantering around with such spirit and pride.

Above left: Monsieur Chapeau surveys the other ponies before joining them in the field

Above right: Monsieur Chapeau and Lady Stumpkin Pumpkin in the pasture

Opposite: Monsieur Chapeau gallops out into the pasture

Right: Monsieur Chapeau making a submissive gesture to Holtball Baluran as he worked his way into the herd

Opposite, clockwise from top: Monsieur Chapeau, second from right, with the herd and putting Holtball Baluran in his place behind him; boisterous colt play between Imperial Topaz and Holtball Baluran; Monsieur Chapeau quickly learned how to get out of trouble

After a fairly short time, he'd clearly run out of steam and had no objection to walking with us back to the barn for a rest, accompanied by a loyal Pumpkin. It was quite enough for one day and he was a tired but very happy chap.

This routine continued over the next few days – with some turnout and then back to the barn – and his fitness steadily increased. Slowly but surely we could see the return of *the joie de vivre* that this little chap must have enjoyed as a healthy foal, before being separated from his mother and herd. The time spent out with the other foals was a wonderful tonic for Monsieur Chapeau.

Monsieur Chapeau Meets Uncle Harry

While Monsieur Chapeau was enjoying getting to know the herd of foals it was clear that they were much stronger than him. As the colts Imperial Topaz and Holtball Baluran were larger and rather robust in their play, we felt a visitor in the form of our adult moorbred gelding Anchor Strongbow 'Uncle Harry' would help with the socialisation. Harry has, over the years, been babysitter to many newly weaned foals and is a wonderful combination of nurturing and guidance, as required. I introduced Harry to Monsieur Chapeau in the barn where he immediately busied himself with Monsieur Chapeau's haylage pile. MC was a little in awe of this strapping, powerful gelding, but Harry was gentle with him and I could see they were going to get on. When I let them out into the field with the other youngsters Harry decided that Monsieur Chapeau did indeed need to be chaperoned – and they stayed close together as they traversed the pasture. With both Harry and Pumpkin to look after him, Monsieur Chapeau enjoyed his turnout time enormously.

As it turned out, Monsieur Chapeau could look after himself very well. When the colts tried to boss him around, or herd him along, he didn't run away from them. Instead, he delivered a forthright double-barrelled kick towards whichever colt was attempting to dominate him and then immediately dipped his head to eat grass. The clear message was along the lines of, 'I'm not intimidated by you and I'm not looking for a fight, but I will defend myself so butt out'. And they did. This tiny, fluffy and still rather weak little foal was proving to be rather assertive – and adept at herd communications. The larger colts were somewhat surprised – and respectful. As it became clear that he could hold his own amongst the other youngsters, Uncle Harry was able to return to his own herd. Soon it was possible for Monsieur Chapeau to be turned out with the other foals for most of the day – returning to his own enclosure for the night, to ensure he could get his full quota of rest and nutrition.

Below left: Monsieur Chapeau meets Uncle Harry

Opposite and below centre and right: Uncle Harry (Anchor Strongbow) looks after Monsieur Chapeau in the field

Chapter 3

Taming Wild Exmoor Ponies – What are we Dealing With?

The Taming of Anchor Imperial Topaz

The colt Imperial Topaz, who is from the famous Anchor Herd, had also taken a keen interest in what was going on in Monsieur Chapeau's accommodations and he had spent a lot of time at the barn gate watching Monsieur Chapeau and Lady Stumpkin Pumpkin.

Topaz is a beautiful pony, but highly sensitive and wary of human contact. He would explode in panic at even the gentlest attempt to touch him and we were gradually working to build his confidence and trust with gentle interactions at liberty and trying to communicate through a feather duster, which enabled the lightest of touches. On choosing Topaz from the Anchor colt foals back in the autumn, we'd been alerted that his mother was rather wild in nature. Having met her, I had felt a strong connection with this magnificent and beautiful mare and she had given me a few clues regarding how best to deal with her son. First and foremost, was the fact that I would have to find the patience to 'take the time it takes' and work with him at liberty – free of restraint – until he willingly accepted handling.

Forced restraint and coercion-based, negative training of sensitive wild ponies can result in lifelong problems of fear-based explosions and unpredictable 'reactions' rather than calm, considered 'responses'. If we get it wrong during the foal socialisation stage, we can negatively affect the kind of ponies they become as adults. Exmoor ponies are highly intelligent, with an enhanced survival instinct and flight responses. They need to be convinced that it is safe to trust and that is something a handler can't demand if we want the best from them. We have to earn their trust and respect. Both Topaz and his mother Amethyst were highly-motivated to resist being handled and

Opposite: Topaz greeting Dawn gently with his muzzle

31

Left: Imperial Topaz showing his explosive resistance to being lightly touched, even with a feather duster

Below: Dawn tentatively making contact with Topaz with the feather duster

Topaz yawning to release stress

to escape from what they perceived as 'predators' wherever possible. Yet they also both showed definite signs of being interested in making a connection with humans – on their terms – and I was sure that, with the right approach, I could build the most amazing rapport with this lovely colt. At this stage though, it was a mere dream and Topaz was still saying a resolute no to any physical contact at all. While he was always curious and would present his muzzle to sniff you gently, his adrenalin soared at the idea of being touched on his body and deep down, I was wondering how on earth I was going to get him to willingly accept a head collar and grooming! Monsieur Chapeau would prove to be the crucial link.

Topaz, like Pumpkin, spent time intently observing and processing our relaxed interactions with Monsieur Chapeau and I was aware of his fascination as MC lay down and even snoozed while I was grooming him. This undoubtedly helped Topaz start to cross the bridge in allowing himself to trust humans – because where there is interest, there is the opportunity for learning. Most days, I endeavoured to spend a few minutes with Topaz in one of the enclosed areas where we gradually progressed our interactions at liberty. He was always willing to engage with his muzzle and sniff noses incredibly gently without any sign of aggression – as long as I remained still and soft. He was also very responsive to fingertip requests to disengage his quarters and take a step around when I asked him to. And then he would step towards me when I invited him. This willingness to move his feet without alarmingly 'scatting away' or resistantly 'planting his feet' (freezing) was a strong sign that he had great potential as a communicative pony. That is, if we could overcome his fear of being touched.

The Guard Side and the Soft Side

Topaz was much happier to show me his offside and was not so keen to show me his nearside. It's thought that some foals favour presenting one side to potential predators (the guard side) while placing their other side (the soft side) close into their mother while they suckle. If there are distinctive sides like this – and it varies from foal to foal – then it is harder for a human handler to achieve willing contact on the protective side. Topaz appeared to be extremely protective of his nearside to the point where he couldn't even bear me to look at it, while he resisted physical contact on all areas of his body apart from the end of his muzzle. And this was why I was still scratching my head about how to socialise him almost three months after he'd arrived at Holt Ball – we had not progressed much beyond the odd stroke with the feather duster! However, I remembered his beautiful mother and the deeply intelligent and passionate look in her eyes and I knew that when Topaz was ready, he would cross the bridge to me.

Feeling the Fear in a Wild Pony

Topaz taught me how to 'feel the fear' in a wild pony. It's easy to remain detached from core emotions if they are being experienced by someone else. This is how we can go about our daily lives and not take on everyone else's 'emotional baggage'. We can empathise and sympathise without actually feeling another person or animal's core emotions – like pain and fear. But this can also cause us to appear rather insensitive. For example, when someone describes burning their hand on the oven, you say 'ouch' but you can't really 'feel' it, you just know that it hurts so you're sympathetic. It's rather like that with fear. If someone tells you they're afraid of riding a horse, you can be sympathetic but we are protected from feeling their actual emotions – for our own sanity. You can't truly understand how they feel until you feel that same fear. While it's natural, and emotionally sensible, to protect yourself from experiencing the intensity of everyone else's emotions, sometimes in order to truly understand the depths of what a wild animal may be feeling we have to make an effort to feel it ourselves – so we can help them overcome it. Topaz was an excellent teacher in this regard. His fear of being touched was so palpable and so intense that once or twice, when I did brush the feather duster on an area of his body where he really didn't want it, an intense bolt of fear shot through my own body – from him. And it was a shock to realise just how petrified he was of being touched. I knew that to progress through this stage, Topaz had to believe that I was safe and he had to learn to find value in being touched. I had to unlock that understanding and willing participation and help him conquer his fear – or I knew I was going to get nowhere fast.

The Muzzle to Hand Touch – The Kiss

I've mentioned that, while Topaz remained touch resistant, he was prepared to offer me his muzzle and his behaviour highlights one of the most important socialisation moments with wild foals. While they may still be unwilling – and emotionally unable – to allow you to touch their body, often the first physical contact will come from the muzzle. It is a huge step for a wild pony to make willing, physical contact with humans – who they see as predators however gently we present ourselves. That is why they can remain head shy and turn their back end towards you. You may even get a touch on the rump first, before you engage with their muzzle. But if you really want to start to build trust and progress a positive relationship with a wild pony, he needs to offer a willing contact with his muzzle. Topaz demonstrated this with great clarity. At first he would raise his muzzle and tentatively sniff nostrils with me. Eventually, he would move his nose towards my outstretched hand where I had my palm facing downwards and the fingers relaxed, and he'd hover his nose there. One day, he touched the back of my hand with a soft 'nudge' from his muzzle. At this point, he leapt away like he'd had an electric shock. This was the first time that our energy

Pumpkin demonstrating the Muzzle to Hand greeting

fields had physically connected and it was a massive moment for Topaz. I felt a bolt of energy shoot through me as well. Over the next few sessions, Topaz learned to touch my hand with his muzzle and not shoot backwards, and that, together with the gentle nose to nose sniffing, became our greeting. This has been the same with every wild foal – there is a distinct moment where they choose to make that contact from muzzle to your hand. It can be described as a Kiss of greeting from pony to human and it's how I greet every pony daily. They can convey a lot about how they're feeling with the way they greet you with their muzzles – or not.

Learning from Observation

As Topaz continued to watch my relaxed interactions with Monsieur Chapeau, and in turn, Monsieur Chapeau watched my interactions with Topaz, he started to slowly and positively change. It was as if Monsieur Chapeau was calmly lifting and removing some of the layers of Topaz's anxiety and helping him realise that he had nothing to be afraid of – he was 'whispering' to him. It's not comfortable for horses or humans to stay 'adrenalin high' and it takes considerable effort to remain 'up there'. So there is enormous relief in being able to return to an equilibrium and place of inner peace – and I sensed that Topaz was yearning to go there.

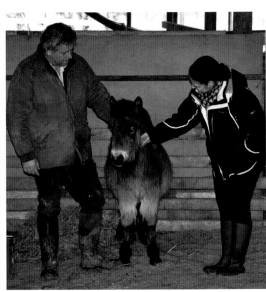

Left to right:
Monsieur Chapeau demonstrating to the other youngsters that he's happy to be handled; Monsieur Chapeau with his visitor Danielle; Monsieur Chapeau with Nick meeting Sue Downes

Monsieur Chapeau had a lot of time to observe the other foals and he missed nothing. He seemed wise beyond his years and this was commented on by the various visitors who came to see him. 'He has such wise eyes, he's like an old soul in a young body' were frequent comments. His plight had caught the public imagination and a constant stream of people dropped by to meet this incredible little pony. He greeted each one with stoic calmness and allowed himself to be stroked and photographed. I got the distinct feeling that Monsieur Chapeau knew he had a very important job to do at Holt Ball.

How Monsieur Chapeau Helped the Other Foals

As Monsieur Chapeau became stronger and more integrated into the foal herd, it meant he could more actively take part in their socialisation sessions. We had created a 15ft x 15ft 'Learning Zone' where the ponies inside could see through the pen to the others in the larger enclosure. I noticed that when I was in the Learning Zone with one or two of the youngsters, some of whom were still very wary of physical contact, Monsieur Chapeau would come and stand close by the pen. He radiated a warm, positive energy and would lower his head slightly, half close his eyes and look like he was dozing. This aura of calmness had a profound effect on the other youngsters and it made my job very much easier. Monsieur Chapeau was clearly communicating to the other ponies that it was OK to trust me and that he was relaxed about the whole process. The ponies in the Learning Zone would often go and stand near to him and sometimes he'd sniff noses with them through the pen. It was here that I could gently approach them and the special atmosphere created by Monsieur Chapeau enabled me to progress with stroking and brushing them, where before they had been more apprehensive. The ponies improved immeasurably and progressed to willingly allowing us to put on head collars, or at least allow body grooming in the case of the rather aloof filly, Farleywater Dazzler.

The special bond created between Monsieur Chapeau and ourselves on the day of his rescue was apparent and whenever I appeared in the pasture, he always came over to say hello – with affection. And he extended this courtesy to anyone who was with me. His curious, trusting nature was showing us that when wild Exmoor ponies are socialised and handled with respect and kindness they are able to extend their trust to humans generally – and to both men and women – and not just one familiar handler.

Monsieur Chapeau lying down centre brings a calmness to the youngstock herd

Progress with Anchor Imperial Topaz

Only a month after Monsieur Chapeau's arrival, and with the benefit of his calming presence, Topaz allowed me to stroke and groom him all over. His fear of humans began to ebb away and one day he let me stroke his neck – an area that had been a complete no-go zone. Shortly after this, he let me gently put on his head collar and it was a special moment when he didn't startle or pull away. He had decided that I could be trusted and once he'd made that decision, he no longer appeared to be nervous. Literally overnight, the fear was gone. To be extended the gift of trust from this previously completely touch-resistant Exmoor pony resonated deeply with all of us involved in the Moorland Exmoor Foal Project. It had taken four and a half months for him to willingly accept a head collar. Topaz was showing us that by taking the time it takes, solid foundations of trust could be established. Just because a pony takes a while to socialise to human contact, it doesn't mean he will be a 'sharp' or nervous pony in the longer term. In fact, Topaz looked like he was going to be the most confident and affectionate pony after Pumpkin and Monsieur Chapeau – and my dream was becoming a reality as his gentle, curious and loving character began to emerge.

Right: Topaz is immensely communicative and keen to engage with his muzzle

Opposite, clockwise from top left:
Topaz willingly accepting a head collar;
Topaz allowing the head collar on;
Topaz shows no fear or tendency to pull away when his head collar is put on;
Topaz overcoming his fear of physical contact and becoming affectionate

Chapter 4

Seeing Things from the Foal's Point of View

When a wild Exmoor pony arrives at Holt Ball, I make every effort to put myself in his (or her) shoes and understand how they may be feeling. Where has this pony come from? What has he left behind and experienced? How does he feel about what's happening to him now? What is his state of mind?

Trying to see it from the pony's point of view can trigger some quite powerful emotions – as Topaz had taught me, you can experience a sharp jolt of the fear or heartache which can radiate from these youngsters. After all, they've just lost the security of their mother, the siblings who they've formed close bonds with, the rest of the herd and their familiar home environment. Their adrenalin is high and their primal survival instinct is acute. The pony does not know if he is going to live or die. Rather than seeing this as a negative, if we can try to understand that these feelings can make it difficult for the foals to trust humans in the early stages, then it reduces the risk of misunderstanding the ponies during socialisation. They are certainly not being 'difficult' or 'naughty' and the last thing they need during this stage is violence, force or coercion from humans.

Horses are gregarious and sociable creatures so even when fearful, they will naturally look to make a connection and reach an understanding with other creatures – because by doing this they have a greater chance of remaining safe. Being accepted within the herd and receiving its protection is key to survival for a horse. So trying to see things from the foal's point of view, and understanding their needs, greatly assists humans with the socialisation of wild ponies – or indeed any unhandled equine youngstock.

Opposite: A multiple hot branded mare who remains difficult and unpredictable, particularly on the branded side

Abrupt Weaning

For semi-feral Exmoor ponies, the 'weaning experience' (separation from their mother) can be dramatic and abrupt. The foal will have been rounded up with his family herd from the open moorland where he has lived wild and free for the first five or six months of his life. The ponies will be gathered in to the home farms, or to holding pens out on the moorland enclosures. No matter how skilfully this is done, the resulting atmosphere amongst the gathered ponies can be electric and fearful, because this is a natural response to being suddenly constrained within a restricted area where escape is not possible. Through previous experience, the older mares will know that it is likely they will lose their foals at this point, although the foal has no idea that he is about to be separated from his mother (*Semi-Feral Weaning* – Koniks: Aleksandra Górecka-Bruzda 2015). What happens to the foal between the point he is separated and the point he arrives at his new home can vary enormously. It is during this period that the foal can receive some 'robust' handling, and whatever he experiences after being rounded up will start to shape the way he views humans thereafter. These experiences can have a profound effect on the pony he will ultimately become. Our quest is to make them as positive as possible.

Multiple Hot Branding

Until very recently, the semi-feral 'wild' Exmoor pony foals were subjected to the practice of multiple hot branding on the shoulder and rump areas, which involved applying up to seven large branded marks with red hot irons, causing the foal to experience severe pain and trauma. The reason for hot branding the foals was to ensure they could be 'visually identified' out on the moor with both herd and individual pony numbers. Until 2014, hot branding was permitted to be used on all Exmoor pony foals, including those leaving the moors and those born into a non-free-living situation – if the owner wished to brand them. To understand the effects of multiple hot branding on the ponies, we need to take a look at what's involved. First the handlers must catch hold of and restrain the foals in what would usually be their first experience of human handling. A head collar is put on and the lead rope tied to or wound around something to secure the head. Some foals will continue to struggle and others will give up and stand fairly still – they will 'freeze'. Two inspectors examine the foal – checking for a correct jaw structure, searching through the mane and tail to spot if there are any white hairs (which are forbidden in the Exmoor breed), and then getting hold of each foot and looking underneath to see if there are any white or pales patches on the undersole or on the hoof wall. Once the inspectors are satisfied that the foal meets the breed standard (a list of required characteristics), a microchip is inserted into the neck by a vet, for individual identification, and around 40 hairs are sharply tugged from the mane or tail complete with follicles, for DNA testing to confirm the foal's parentage. Someone will then clip

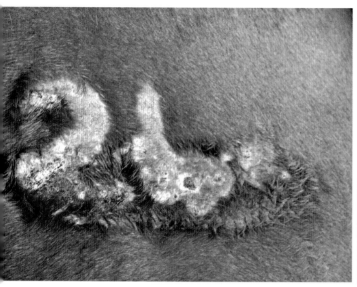
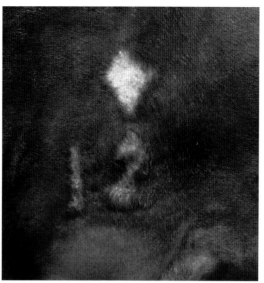
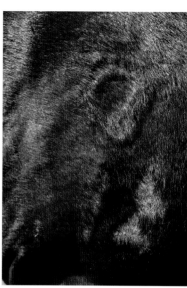

the hair away from the shoulder and rump areas to prepare them for hot branding. There is very little muscle over the shoulder, so the application of a red hot iron for up to four seconds, which causes the equivalent of a third degree human burn (scientifically proven by the University of Veterinary Medicine in Vienna: Erber, Regina, 2012), can result in 'bone pain' which must be excruciating. Firstly, a large diamond-shaped brand is applied to the shoulder – 'the Exmoor pony Star'. While this is sizzling away, the herd number of up to three digits is added underneath it. If the herd number begins with 'H' then this would require a separate, additional brand. And finally, the individual pony number of up to three digits is applied to the rump. By this time the foal would already be suffering from two large third degree burns and as the rump is approached, foals have been known to sink down to the ground in despair. We can't even begin to understand what these foals must experience being repeatedly hot branded like this, but if you've ever burnt your hand on the oven or a woodburner, you'll have an inkling of what it must feel like. Especially if someone then wanted to burn your other hand too. A particularly queasy part of this process is that the equipment used to heat up the branding irons can be rather basic and sometimes they are not heated up enough. This can result in the re-heated irons having to be re-applied to a partially burned brand to complete the job. At this point, especially if it's repeated to various brands on the same foal, they can literally go berserk with the pain. I've witnessed this process a number of times and, especially given that the resulting brands are often indecipherable, have been moved to campaign strongly to stop the practice.

Left to right: A deep hot brand which continued to open up and bleed on this pony when she was three years old; a severe Exmoor pony 'star' brand which was so deep that the hair follicles have completely died in the centre of the diamond; a herd number brand which has clearly 'slid' when applied showing a skewed '2' and which causes flaking of the skin all year round

Mental Trauma of Anticipation

Another consideration is the mental stress experienced by foals waiting for their turn to be hot branded and watching the procedure being carried out on their siblings. Given that horses learn through observation and are intelligent creatures, it is likely that the last foal to be hot branded experiences far greater trauma than the first foal through the anticipation of what is about to happen.

Arguments attempting to justify the practice include claims that the Exmoor pony has 'thicker skin' than other equine breeds and that the practice simply 'doesn't hurt them'. This is incorrect and it has been scientifically proven that the top layer of the epidermis (skin) of a horse actually contains more nerve endings than even human skin. ('Horse Whipping Report' – Dr Lydia Tong MA VetMB Veterinary Pathologist, NSW Department of Primary Industries.)

Other arguments suggest that because the foals often return to grazing or eating forage after hot branding, this means they are unconcerned about the practice. However studies have shown that when a horse experiences pain or trauma, their natural survival instinct causes them to try to appear as unconcerned as possible, so they don't attract the attention of predators – who are generally intent on picking out the weakest horse from the herd to target for food. So just because a pony is 'quiet' after hot branding does not necessarily mean he is feeling 'fine'. He may just be trying to survive and making every attempt to conceal his distress. Horses and ponies also don't scream like dogs and cats and people do, and I do wonder if multiple hot branding would have continued to be practiced for so long if they did.

If branded too deeply, the scars can continue to burst open in places even when the pony is an adult, especially during hot weather, and they can bleed and cause irritation and itching. Generally, the brands cause unsightly flaking skin in the branded area thereafter. Some experts feel that the practice can 'fuse' skin to the muscle and cause a resistant 'dragging' of the skin in that area, resulting in an unpleasant sensation for the pony when moving. Various ponies are subsequently reactive, fearful and even aggressive to people moving in to the branded side which can be alarming – and dangerous.

In short, hot branding causes extreme pain and the repeated application of red hot irons to a restrained foal can be described as torture. The practice was used as a 'medieval torture' which highlights its severity. In my opinion, repeatedly hot branding previously unhandled foals is barbaric.

Working to Bring an End to Hot Branding of Ponies

Hot branding is considered by many to cause 'unnecessary suffering' (which is illegal under the Animal Welfare Act 2006 and its accompanying regulations) and the practice is banned in Scotland and Ireland, although it is still practiced in England and Wales. All Exmoor pony foals are now routinely microchipped for individual identification and it is a fact that hot branded marks can be notoriously difficult to read on their thick coats. In 2014, the British government (DEFRA) thankfully introduced a Code of Practice which has restricted hot branding to the rump area, and to only be used on semi-feral foals returning to a free-living situation. Foals leaving the moors, or those born 'in ground' in a domestic situation, are no longer permitted to be hot branded. Work continues to reduce the number of branded marks from four to a single mark, and to find a suitable alternative form of visual identification for semi-feral ponies, so the practice can be eradicated entirely. Unfortunately there is currently no suitable alternative – collars come off and can get hung up on things, the long-range microchip reader has not yet been developed, ear-tagging is unpleasant (and illegal), paint marks rub off, freeze-branding is felt to be unsuitable for unhandled foals, and mane and tail cutting is impractical and temporary. So, despite the reduction in the number of brands allowed, the Exmoor pony is still the most heavily hot branded animal on the planet.

How Unreadable Hot Brands can Cause Registration Problems

Hot branding as a method of visual identification has been responsible for the loss of some good moorland Exmoor ponies from the breeding gene pool. The branded marks can sometimes not be successfully deciphered and this failure to correctly identify mares through brands alone (ie, if they are older mares and not microchipped) has resulted in various anomalies in the DNA parentage verification source data – causing some foals to be excluded from pedigree registration despite meeting the breed standard and being deemed to be of suitable quality. With a dangerously small gene pool, the unreliability of hot branding as a form of visual identification has proved to be catastrophic at times, as a management tool for this endangered breed.

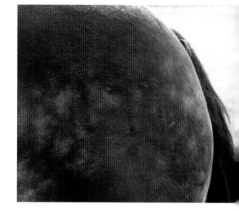

An example of a not so easy to read brand and this is on a smooth summer coat where it should be clear

Working Towards Better Welfare – and Wellbeing – for Exmoor Ponies

None of the Exmoor foals who join the Moorland Exmoor Foal Project have been hot branded and this is a blessing. However, most of them have experienced forced restraint during the inspection process. This is obviously not as traumatic as being hot branded at the same time. However, the process can instil a fear of restraint and enhance the ponies' wariness of humans which has to be overcome during their subsequent socialisation. We have noticed that wild Exmoor pony foals who

Moorland Exmoor Foal Project foals who are all unbranded and experiencing better welfare through sensitive handling

have not undergone forced restraint as their first experience of human contact are usually easier to socialise. The quest continues to improve the management and handling of Exmoor ponies when they are gathered in from the moors. This is a core objective of the Exmoor farmers and land owners who are working together in the Moorland Exmoor Pony Breeders Group (MEPBG) to facilitate improved breeding practices and management for Moorland Exmoor ponies.

Exmoor Ponies and Their Reputation for Being 'Difficult'

As well as being treasured as a beautiful indigenous 'wild' native pony breed, Exmoor ponies have long had a reputation for being rather difficult, flighty and 'quirky' to handle and ride, with a tendency to exhibit unpredictable and sometimes explosive behaviours. Although many Exmoor ponies are adored by their owners and excel in various performance spheres – from agility and driving, to showing, jumping and endurance – there are too many tales of woe from people who've experienced erratic behaviour from their Exmoor ponies to deny there is a problem. We need to take a long hard look at the causes and the effects – and it may well be that this is through no fault of the ponies. These undesirable behaviours can range from the ponies being hard to catch, defensive and over-anxious, or demonstrating a tendency to bolt, kick, bite, buck, tank off while being led, etc. Many times, when I've mentioned Exmoor ponies a person's eyes will widen as they recount the tales of 'the Exmoor pony they had as a child'. While these tales can be amusing and entertaining on one hand, the common denominator is an Exmoor pony with enhanced fear or anger-based responses which may have resulted from a traumatic start in life – or rather, trauma experienced when they start life off the moors.

Being the owner of some seven hot branded Exmoor ponies and over twenty unbranded Exmoors, I can categorically say there is a significant difference in the attitude, ability to trust, confidence and behaviours of branded ponies compared to unbranded ones. While Exmoor ponies display a wide range of individual characters – ranging from very shy to bold and confident – there is no doubt in my mind that the negative effects of multiple hot branding adds an undesirable 'potency' and 'edge' to their reasoning and reactions. This can be exacerbated by ongoing handling which involves force and coercion.

'Swinging' and Other 'Socialisation' Techniques for Wild Foals

The reputation of the Exmoor pony for being difficult may also have been assisted by some of the more robust 'socialisation' practices, several of which are still unfortunately practised today. For some foals, being 'tamed' is not an entirely pleasant experience, and some people advocate shutting the wild foal in a stable for at least a month, often with the top door closed so they won't jump out. What happens then can vary – some endeavour to tame the foal by sitting with it in the stable, while others will get hold of the foal, put on a head collar and tie him up to something that 'won't break' like a ring in the wall or to a pillar. They'll leave the foal to thrash about and 'head collar train himself'. This can take a few days and some forage and water is put within reach while the foal tries to free himself and eventually gives up. Once the foal stands quietly, he is considered to be 'head collar trained' or 'halter broken'. This is called 'swinging'.

Top: The wary and somewhat hostile expression that can occur frequently in some hot branded ponies

Above: Exmoors have acquired a reputation for sometimes being difficult to handle

Following this, some people leave the head collar on the foal, with a rope trailing from it which the foal can step on whenever he lowers his head, delivering a sharp jerk to his head as he tries to lift it again. While the handler may find this convenient for 'getting hold of the foal when desired' or 'teaching the foal to respect the rope', it can leave the foal with a dislike of the whole process, including the head collar and rope, and it is no surprise when he is 'difficult to catch' when let out into the field thereafter – sometimes for the rest of his life. Some 'leading training' can consist of wrestling with the foal on the rope using brute force until he leads along with the handler. Suffice it to say, we do not approve of such methods of foal training at Holt Ball and instead encourage the use of positive, trust-based handling. By positive, I mean a 'positive, kind attitude' which uses 'yes' and 'no' with the aim of building trust – not achieving objectives through coercion, and force.

How Monsieur Chapeau Showed what Exmoors can Really be Like

By falling ill and weak out on the moor and becoming separated from his mother and herd, Monsieur Chapeau had experienced none of the practices described above. He had not been rounded up, forcibly restrained, hot branded, abruptly weaned from his mother by humans, shut away in a dark stable and 'swung' to head collar 'break' him. While he had endured incredible natural hardship that had placed him close to not surviving at all, he did not associate humans with it. So his first main contact with people, other than seeing them out and about on the moor, was to save his life, not threaten it or cause him pain. And because of that, he has been able to demonstrate what it is possible to achieve with regard to establishing an early connection of trust and friendship with a wild Exmoor foal. While dealing with a foal in a weakened state is very different to dealing with a healthy foal able to engage his full flight responses, there is still much we can learn from our interactions with Monsieur Chapeau, and apply that to the way we work with and socialise wild ponies. He has brought a new level of understanding and awareness to the Moorland Exmoor Foal Project which is greatly assisting in helping the ponies to build trust with us. And he is teaching us the language of 'pony whispering'.

Monsieur Chapeau is keen to be friends with everyone

A Natural Desire to be our Friend

It is truly amazing how quickly the wild ponies will try to adapt to their new surroundings and forge social relationships with new companions – and with humans – and here lies the main reason that the intense bond of love between man and horse has endured through the ages. Horses are intelligent, sociable creatures who are generous of spirit and incredibly forgiving of our clumsiness, lack of mindfulness and understanding and sometimes unintentional thoughtlessness.

Monsieur Chapeau has developed a close bond of trust with Dawn

Winston Churchill said that, 'The outside of a horse is good for the inside of a man.' And he was right. They also offer the most wonderful opportunity for experiencing unconditional love, self-improvement and positive development of character. In short, horses and particularly wild Exmoor ponies can enrich our lives and souls — if we treat them well.

Chapter 5

Connecting with Wild Foals at Liberty to Build Trust

We like to start our interactions with wild foals at liberty, where they are loose and free to walk away if they feel uncomfortable. For a wild foal, just being in the same enclosure with a human can feel like 'restraint' and it takes time for them to shrink the 'pressure' zone around them and willingly allow us into their space. An understanding of these zones is vital when taming wild ponies.

The 'Zones' Around a wild pony – Awareness, Influence and Pressure

Out on the moor, wild ponies will become aware of the presence of people when they're far away on the horizon. They will carry on doing what they're doing until the human reaches a distance that they feel may potentially compromise their safety. This can be hundreds of metres in some cases, depending on the individual pony or the 'herd energy'. As the human advances from what has been the ponies' 'Zone of Awareness' into the 'Zone of Influence' they get ready to make a response. This may involve gently migrating away from the human or it may involve taking flight to what they perceive is a safe distance. Some ponies will allow a human to advance to within a few feet, before moving away. This depends very much on the energy and intent of the human. The immediate area around a pony is known as the 'Pressure Zone' and it's worth bearing in mind that, as a prey animal, the Exmoor pony's survival mechanism is first to run, until running is not an option – and then to fight. In times gone by, wild ponies would have been hunted by larger animals for food (wolves, big cats, etc). These predators would single out what they perceived to be a weaker pony and at the point of contact, they would sink their claws or teeth into the pony

Monsieur Chapeau snoozing across Dawn's lap with Imperial Topaz and Farleywater Scarlet looking on

and try to bring him down to the ground. Rather like what you see leopards doing to wildebeest out on the African plains. At this point, if the pony continues to run, he risks his flesh being torn away, so he will stop and fight – using his teeth and hooves to do what he can to dislodge and repel the predator. In this 'Zone of Pressure' he will push back into and towards the predator with the aim of pressuring the predator to release his teeth or claws, so he has a chance to escape, or disable the predator. This is often the horse's last resort when under attack.

Although Exmoor ponies are no longer hunted for food by wild predators, these Zones of Awareness, Influence and Pressure remain. And this is why a pony will watch someone approach from a certain distance, make the decision to move away at a certain point when they get nearer, and then possibly advance towards them if he finds himself in a contained space in close proximity with 'a predator', and considers that there is a threat to his safety. When working with wild foals, it is very important to be mindful and acutely aware of these zones around the pony and understand the reactions and responses that are natural for the pony to offer. The socialisation process depends on clarity of communication both ways, between human and pony, and the ability to build trust through fair and reasonable interactions, where both handler and pony feel safe.

Stags within the ponies' Zone of Influence

Opposite: The Farleywater H67 herd migrating across the huge expanse of Brendon Common demonstrate the range of the ponies' 'Zone of Awareness'

A pony may decide to defend himself from within the Pressure Zone

Right: These ponies have made the decision to take flight

Allowing a Wild Foal to Retreat

Absolutely key to the initial interactions with a wild Exmoor foal is to allow the foal to move away from you if he needs to. It may only be a few paces if you're working in an enclosure, but even within a contained space, if the foal feels he can 'retreat', without you constantly 'advancing' towards him, he will feel safer. If you have a foal in a head collar and on a rope during these first interactions, the foal has no choice but to stay with you, and if he tries to leave he meets the force of restraint. From here the seeds of fear, anxiety and resistance are sown. However, if the foal can retreat and approach as he needs to and you can adjust and time your approaches and retreats according to the signals he gives you, he learns that this is a two-way communication process in which he has choices and the opportunity to express his feelings. From these early liberty connections, the seeds of trust, confidence and friendship are sown – which will lay positive, solid foundations for the pony's lifetime.

Monsieur Chapeau Shows us What can be Achieved with Kindness

By offering his immediate trust from the first day of meeting us, Monsieur Chapeau had 'raised the bar' of what could be achieved. It was a great reassurance for us to know that it was indeed possible to willingly handle and positively interact with a wild foal almost immediately after bringing him in off the moor. We now needed to learn from this and improve our horsemanship to become better at winning the trust of the wild foals who were more energetic, naturally resistant and 'flighty' when they arrived with us. I felt Monsieur Chapeau had arrived at Holt Ball to offer us a Master Class in foal socialisation and pony whispering techniques!

Monsieur Chapeau loves to sleep while he's being brushed

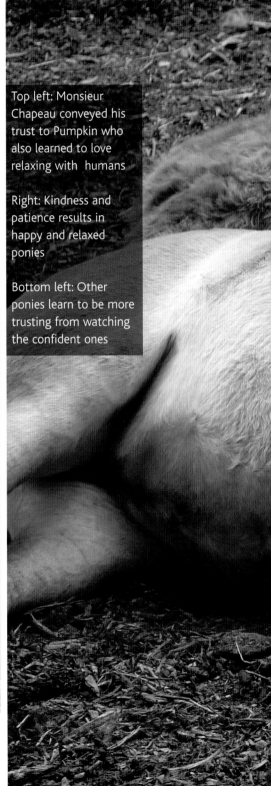

Top left: Monsieur Chapeau conveyed his trust to Pumpkin who also learned to love relaxing with humans

Right: Kindness and patience results in happy and relaxed ponies

Bottom left: Other ponies learn to be more trusting from watching the confident ones

Below left to right: Monsieur Chapeau and Pumpkin were first on the tarpaulin; Pumpkin conveys confidence to the more wary ponies

Opposite, clockwise from top left: Topaz really wants to join Pumpkin on the tarpaulin; Topaz leading the other foals through the drums; Pumpkin demonstrating a lovely 'draw to me'; Pumpkin explores the giant green ball; Monsieur Chapeau and Pumpkin

Monsieur Chapeau Discovers Agility

At Holt Ball, our goal is to create a natural, calm environment where the foals can live within a sibling herd. Central to both their herd and human interactions is the opportunity to explore and play. As with all species, 'play' stimulates rapid learning as it invites willing participation, the opportunity to be creative and to have freedom of expression. Ponies are highly intelligent and when you engage their interest and allow them to think for themselves by introducing enjoyable objects and tasks, their understanding and development accelerates – which builds their confidence – and their trust in you.

The Moorland Exmoor Foal Project youngsters had become closely bonded and while we continued with their individual socialisation sessions to get them used to wearing head collars and accepting basic necessities such as handling and grooming, there were also opportunities to play with them as a herd. With his calm and trusting nature Monsieur Chapeau helped the other more wary foals to engage with us and we had fun introducing them to some of the agility obstacles. These included brightly-coloured tarpaulins, big blue plastic drums, tyres, a flapping plastic curtain, coloured poles, a giant green ball, and a big podium made out of a tractor tyre. These objects offered the ponies the opportunity to explore different colours, shapes and surfaces – where they could walk over, around and through exciting and unusual things that sometimes moved and rustled in the breeze. Exmoor ponies encounter a wide range of natural obstacles and stimulus out

on their moorland enclosures when they're born wild and free – and exploration, play and working out what's safe and what isn't comes very naturally to them.

At first, the other ponies took their lead from Monsieur Chapeau, watching intently as he and Lady Stumpkin Pumpkin boldly walked across the tarpaulin – seemingly more concerned with being the first onto it than worried about what it was. Soon the bolder youngsters were enthusiastically exploring, while the more wary ponies looked on and processed everything that was happening. They would tentatively approach an obstacle like the tarpaulin and sniff at it. These shyer ponies tended to watch the others the first time, think about it all afterwards, and have a go the next time. It was a great way of interacting and bonding with them – and it gave interesting insights into their characters. For example, while filly Farleywater Dazzler remained wary of handling, when it came to exploring the agility objects, she was extremely bold and often one of the first to try things out. This showed me that her reluctance to engage with us was due to her leadership qualities rather than timidity. And while Farleywater Firestar kept back behind the others, she seemed determined to have a go – and during one session, when three of the ponies had followed me through two blue drums, I turned around to see Firestar darting through as if to say 'look, I can do it too!' Certainly, the interactions during these play sessions helped me to understand the ponies' characters better and progressed our relationship with them.

Establishing a Heart Centre Connection

One of the first things I'm looking to establish with wild foals is a 'connection'. This isn't a physical connection, like having the pony on a rope. It's a connection of 'energy' between the handler and pony, rather like being 'plugged in' – where a clear line of communication is open and receptive between you. At first a wild pony's adrenalin can be high and his attention is preoccupied with how he might escape and 'leave the situation'. He can appear distracted and unwilling to focus on the handler. As he becomes calmer and more confident, he is then able to start taking an interest in the handler and offering his attention. At this stage the attention the pony offers can be brief and sporadic, with any sudden noise or movement – or mistake on the part of the handler – breaking the connection and distracting him. Ponies can be very shy and quick to turn their heads away, or move away, at this stage. The distinct feeling you can get is 'please will you just go away or let me out of here – I want to be with the others'. With socialisation, we're looking to turn that desire to escape into willing engagement and trust, where the pony becomes confident with us in his proximity and even finds contact with humans pleasurable. Endeavouring to establish a warm connection emanating from the handler's 'heart centre' to the ponies' heart centre is important, before making any attempt to actually touch the pony.

The best way I can describe this is if you imagine being in a room with a stranger who you're not at all sure of, and they suddenly walk across the room and grab you and start trying to make you move around. Compare that to a stranger standing over on the other side of the room, in a relaxed manner, making friendly eye contact with you but not staring, breathing easily and expressing non-confrontational body language. And then, when he senses you're accepting of his presence, taking a step or two towards you and pausing. Which stranger would you feel more comfortable being in close proximity to? Exactly. So in a socialisation session with a wild pony, I will make every effort to pause, be relaxed and convey that I mean no harm and am not intending to 'pounce' on or lunge at the pony. I try to give him time to process this, assess me, assess the 'risk' and come to the conclusion that our interaction is going to be safe. As we're not communicating with speech, the pony needs to 'feel it'. Just as I will be reading his 'energy' and being aware of any rise in adrenalin that may result in an 'explosive' movement, he is also reading me to assess if my energy levels are remaining calm, and therefore, not likely to result in 'aggressive predatory behaviour'. Radiating a genuine feeling of warmth and good intention towards the pony and inviting him to acknowledge and 'connect' to that intention can result in vastly increased understanding between handler and pony.

Monsieur Chapeau proved to be a great help in improving connection with the ponies. His willingness to convey affection and reassurance to the other ponies was extraordinary and he helped me to understand the importance of establishing a clear and well-intentioned connection before attempting physical contact.

Being in the Present Moment

Being in the 'here and now' helps to make a successful connection with a pony. It's not ideal to start any interaction in a distracted state – thinking about the next supermarket shop, job and lifestyle issues, or anything else that occupies the human mind, especially if it's stressful. Busy, distracted thoughts create 'noise' and can result in a rather chaotic and confusing 'energy' around a person, which can be alarming to a pony, particularly a wild one. Concentrating on being in the present moment reassures the pony, because if a person is calm and focused and listening, they're less likely to behave in a thoughtless, unpredictable, reactive and therefore, potentially unsafe way. We humans are susceptible to letting our minds flit about all over the place and horses are very good at teaching us to quieten our minds, focus and pay attention – in that state, it's easier to progress willing communication and participation with a pony. 'Pony whispering' can actually be well described as 'calmly listening to the pony'.

Teaching the 'Draw to Me'

One of the core principles of socialising ponies at liberty is establishing the 'Draw to Me' which I touched on in the work I'd been doing with Topaz. Teaching a pony to respond to an invitation to move his feet and walk towards me, and 'come to me' ultimately means that at any time the pony gets loose – or I need to let him go for whatever reason – he will be more inclined to come back to me than run away. This is a powerful stage in the socialisation process because ponies are flight animals and their natural inclination is to move away to a position of safety. By choosing to walk willingly towards a handler, they are acknowledging that there is trust and that they feel safer being with the handler than retreating somewhere else. This is something I like to establish with the wild foals as soon as possible, and certainly before a head collar is introduced. Having the 'Draw to Me' connection brings great reassurance to pony and handler – because at the end of the day, the ponies are far stronger than us and realistically, if they want to get away, no rope can hold them. However, if the connection and understanding is there, the rope isn't needed for restraint – only for reassuring communication.

The 'Draw to Me' starts with inviting the pony to take a look towards me. Wild foals will often turn their head away from the handler and 'hide'. A very shy foal will turn his back end to the handler and bury his face in the corner of the enclosure. As they become more confident and realise that we're not going to 'grab' them, they start to glance around. The moment I'm looking for is when I pause near to a foal and the foal realises I've stopped and slightly turns his head to look at me. At that point I will gently sway or step away again. This often causes the foal to turn his head more towards me. He soon learns that by giving me his attention, he can 'stop' me – and even make me 'go away'. At this early stage, the greatest reward I can give a foal is to go away. They are not interested in food treats or being stroked – they just want to be free from the situation. What we're trying to establish when the foal is in this very early stage of being tamed, is that two-way communication is possible. There is a palpable relief which flows through the foal when he realises that he's being listened to and a receptive foal will quickly pick all of this up. As their understanding and confidence increases that I will 'follow the rules' and stop or move away when they look at me, there is a moment when I will gently invite them with my fingers to draw to me and take a step towards me. When that happens, this willing step is symbolic, because a major advancement in their socialisation has taken place.

Monsieur Chapeau picked this up extremely quickly and was happy to draw to me almost immediately – as soon as his little legs were strong enough. When he joined the other ponies, the strength and clarity of his 'Draw to Me' was astounding, He taught me that I could connect with a pony in amongst the herd and ask that pony to draw out from the group and come to me – and

then go into another enclosure. The herd would come in from the pasture and MC would be milling around with them. I'd make eye contact with him, say his name and then invite him to come to me and go into his area. He'd acknowledge my request and then do it. And so would Pumpkin. Although I'd been moving and herding ponies around for years, the sheer sentient clarity of these interactions with Monsieur Chapeau brought things to a new level and I realised these ponies were capable of much more subtle communications and responses than I'd given them credit for.

I should mention here that in the previous few years, I'd formed a very close bond with our Exmoor stallion, Hawkwell Versuvius 'Bear' and together we had won two world championships in International Horse Agility. Bear had learned to navigate complex courses of obstacles and challenges at liberty, both in the arena and out in wilderness areas, and the connection I enjoyed with him was incredible. He has been the most amazing teacher and as a stallion, requires the utmost respect and consideration in order to motivate him to willingly participate. When I started

Above: Topaz drawing to me through the narrow gap of blue barrels
Below: Stallion Hawkwell Versuvius 'Bear'

to socialise Bear as a foal, he had significant fear-based issues to overcome and had been multiple hot branded. That is another whole story. Building on the work I'd done with Bear, the foal project was now offering yet more opportunities in learning how to connect with wild ponies in a herd situation – with the advantage of being able to build trust from the beginning, rather than having to overcome trauma first. And the positive differences in starting from this 'blank canvas' were already becoming glaringly obvious.

The 'Send Away'

Once a pony is comfortable drawing to me, the next thing I work on is the 'Send Away' – the reverse gesture – where the pony learns to step away from me. This isn't a 'send away' in the sense of chasing the pony or causing a reactive scattering of steps. It is establishing the understanding to take one, simple slow step away on a gentle request (like a slow flutter of fingers). When you have a 'draw' and a 'send' – with the head, shoulders and hind quarters – you suddenly have steering, which has been achieved through willing participation. This is the basis for all liberty work, and translates well into leading and later on, riding. A pony who can respond to the draw and send, from a distance, without restraint, is a joy to handle and you never have to worry about them 'getting loose' because they will always respond to you. It is also very useful in calling ponies in from the pasture. They can read fingertip signals from as far away as they are able to see.

A Word About Hand Fed 'Treats' as Rewards

Although there are many different methods and ways to work with ponies, ours does not involve routinely feeding treats from the hand. I find that the use of food is best kept to specific 'feed times', rather than fed continuously through a training session as 'treat rewards'. For example, I'll often give a small feed when I call them in from the pasture (and this may even be forage rather than hard feed) and I'll give a small feed after a training session – from a bowl or on the ground for individuals and small groups, or again perhaps forage for large groups. When I'm dealing with herds of upwards of ten young ponies, I don't want them looking to my pockets for treats when I'm walking in amongst them. Exmoor ponies love their food and it's great to utilise this enthusiasm – we just prefer not to give it to them from our hands. I've found this results in less nipping, barging and frustrated behaviours as the ponies are not accustomed to 'demanding' treats. Although I appreciate that some horsemanship methods, like clicker training, incorporate ways of teaching a horse not to demand the treats, there is an added dimension when dealing with large herds of wild foals and youngstock – and we've found that simply removing the hand fed treats is fundamentally safer.

Teaching the Pasture Recall

When dealing with a largish herd of wild Exmoor youngsters it's important that they get plenty of turnout in the pasture. They're used to living wild and free on large expanses of moorland that can sometimes span thousands of acres. It must be difficult for them to find themselves restricted to small spaces and this is why our system doesn't involve them being shut into individual stables, unless they need to be separated for veterinary reasons. We have therefore created a natural management system with access to barns, corrals and the pasture – where the herds can migrate in and out largely at will. However, if you let a herd of wilful youngsters gallop around the pasture, you need to be sure you can get them in again – and when you want to!

We teach the moorland foals to come in from the pasture when asked

As their trust builds, the youngsters become curious and keen to connect and confident to come to the call

Worming Before Turnout

As soon as a new Moorland youngster arrives at Holt Ball, they're introduced to forage in the form of hay or haylage, which they tend to accept straightaway. Slightly more difficult can be the introduction of a feed bowl, as they simply don't understand what it is at first. Some foals catch on quickly and thoroughly enjoy their food and others can take a week or so to show interest. As soon as they start enjoying a small feed, we can worm them and this is extremely important as foals coming off the moors usually arrive with a significant ascarid burden. These nasty worms can really try them and at around eight months old, the pony will start to build up a natural immunity to them. However, before that it can be a serious problem and we're keen to deal with the worms before they go out onto the pasture. So a new foal will spend a few days in the barn and corral area before going out with the others. During this time before worming, a little initial socialisation takes place and I will endeavour to achieve the basic 'draw to me' even if the foal is still unwilling to be physically touched. Once this crucial understanding is achieved, the foal can go out into the pasture – where they will quickly learn from the other foals how the pasture recall works.

When I want to teach pasture recall, I'll usually prepare a small feed for everyone and then go and ask them to come in. It's advisable to do it when the foals are most likely to want to come in and therefore the request has a pleasant association. So, for example, late afternoon is a good time, when there's a natural desire to come back into the barn and corral for something nice to eat. If some ponies hang back, it's usually only for a few minutes as their desire to be with the rest of the herd is generally stronger than their desire to stay out alone. It can require some patience in the initial stages in allowing time for the stragglers to come in. As their responses get better, I start calling them in at different times of the day, for example, if we want to do some socialisation sessions. They then get used to coming in, having a small feed and being let out again. As time progresses, the herd learns to respond to a call and will come in on request and go out again easily, at any time of the day or night. And they learn to do it without necessarily always having a feed – although I would ensure there's some fresh haylage for them to enjoy, so that there is always a pleasant association for coming in. The ponies enjoy these interactions and are interested to come in because they are naturally sociable creatures. This ability to respond to a recall at liberty, without the need for 'catching' or 'herding' them in establishes strong foundations which will last a lifetime – and makes management of the ponies, and moving the ponies, much easier. This is also very handy if ponies inadvertently escape from a pasture which has been known to happen.

Of course, when Monsieur Chapeau arrived, the pasture recall was vastly improved because he and Lady Stumpkin Pumpkin would always be keen to come to me whenever I appeared. As was Anchor Imperial Topaz. As time progressed I found that I could appear at the gate any time of day or evening and they would always come in even in the dark. The connection with our pony herds has developed to a degree where the ponies are actually joyful to see you and will always respond to the call. It has never failed to move me when I see them either cantering in, or migrating across the pasture in a relaxed way – either way, it's a willing decision to come in.

Top: As the youngsters mature, their pasture recalls are joyful

Above: Sometimes they'll canter and sometimes they'll walk – but they'll always come in

Chapter 6

Spring to Summer – Who is Monsieur Chapeau?

Monsieur Chapeau's Incredible Coat Change!

As Monsieur Chapeau's first spring at Holt Ball approached, he started to shed his incredible winter coat – shedding is activated by increased daylight hours so can start quite early in the year.

As Exmoors have a thick, double-layered coat that protects them against the harshest weather conditions, the brushing and grooming seemed endless. Monsieur Chapeau still had a mass of dreadlocks under his belly that were only going to be dislodged with a coat change, and he fortunately enjoyed being brushed very much. With lots of grooming and rolling, the gradual removal of his vast coat began to hint at a very nice pony underneath and it was heartening to see how his previously malnourished body was beginning to recover and gain condition. During

Opposite: Reaching the spot gets Monsieur Chapeau's approval

Left to right: Monsieur Chapeau going through his coat change; Monsieur Chapeau had a lot of hair to shed; enjoying a roll while he has his tummy brushed

this period he went through some amusing stages, including a few days when he sported a pair of incredibly fluffy knees and fetlocks on otherwise smooth legs, making him look like he was wearing 1970s fancy dress. The hair shedding from Monsieur Chapeau and the other ponies looked like it might feather the nests of most of the birds on Exmoor!

Top: A complete scruff ball mid coat change

Above: Monsieur Chapeau going through an interesting stage with Farleywater Firestar on the right

Right: Monsieur Chapeau modelling his incredible fluffy knees

Monsieur Chapeau is Microchipped, Gelded and DNA Tested

By now Monsieur Chapeau had gained enough muscle condition to be microchipped. All equines in the UK must have a microchip placed in the neck so they can be individually identified and when vet Simon arrived from Western Counties Equine Hospital, Monsieur Chapeau was lying down having a rest in the barn. He saw no reason to get up and therefore had his microchip inserted while he remained lying down, which amused Simon. When his DNA hair sample was taken, which requires around forty tail hairs to be pulled out with their root follicles (DNA parentage verification is a requirement for Exmoor pony registration) he stood calmly and only gave a few flicks of his eyes as if to say, 'Er, I'm not too keen on this.' A brave little chap. As Monsieur Chapeau was running with a herd of fillies as well as colts, it was decided to geld him along with the other colts. When the day came, the vet felt it would be kinder for him to have a full anaesthetic and so Monsieur Chapeau knew nothing at all about the process, spending the whole time asleep in a big, comfortable straw bed. The boys were given plenty of pain relief for a couple of weeks afterwards and all made a speedy and complete recovery. Monsieur Chapeau's lovely temperament remained unchanged and he didn't seem to mind at all.

The Arrival of Farleywater Tom Faggus and Annie Ridd

May brought the arrival of two more Farleywater yearlings who had managed to evade the pony gathering on Buscombe the previous autumn and had stayed out on the moor for the winter. As a result they were both naturally weaned from their mothers and were in a predicament as a home was required for them immediately – and it is not always easy to find a good home for wild yearlings. Their DNA parentage verification was likely to take some time as they had been separated from their mothers, which held the risk that they would not be able to be registered as pedigree ponies. We were impressed with their quality – they had the distinct 'stamp' of the other ten Farleywater foals we had taken into the Moorland Exmoor Foal Project, so we decided to offer them an opportunity at Holt Ball. The colt, Tom Faggus (named after the charismatic highwayman in *Lorna Doone* who managed to evade capture for a long time) had to be gelded soon after arrival so he could run safely with the fillies. However, this gave him a much needed chance in life and he was soon out with the rest of the herd. We looked forward to registering both Tom Faggus and Annie Ridd as pedigree Exmoor ponies.

Annie Ridd and Tom Faggus integrating into the herd with Farleywater Dazzler establishing the ground rules

From Fluff Ball to a Rather Smart Pony – But who is Monsieur Chapeau?

With the arrival of early summer, Monsieur Chapeau finally shed the last remnants of his winter coat and revealed a rather gorgeous, sleek and beautifully-shaped pony underneath. We were all amazed at his exceptionally pretty head and compact, well-conformed body, with strong, stocky little legs. No one had really known what to expect the day we brought the emaciated, bedraggled little foal in from the moor. It was a wonderful surprise to discover that Monsieur Chapeau was turning out to be such a handsome pony with very nice conformation. And looking at his lovely condition now it was hard to guess that just six months previously he had been so close to death. But who is Monsieur Chapeau – which herd was he born into and who are his parents? These were questions we were keen to have answered.

As all Exmoor ponies born out on the moors in free-living herds are required to have their parentage (mother and father) verified, Monsieur Chapeau's DNA sample had been sent off to the Exmoor Pony Society along with his microchip information. We were looking forward to hearing the results so he could have his physical inspection. He could then hopefully go to a show or two and help promote the breed – as he was looking like show quality.

Opposite: Annie Ridd and Tom Faggus meeting some of the herd – Farleywater Dazzler, Firestar and Imperial Topaz

Below left: Monsieur Chapeau with Miriam Main, revealing his very pretty head as well as his fondness for being scratched on the neck

Below right: The handsome Monsieur Chapeau

Disaster! Monsieur Chapeau Cannot be Called an Exmoor pony?

We waited in anticipation to hear the results from the Exmoor Pony Society DNA parentage test, but after some weeks, there was great disappointment when the society said that Monsieur Chapeau's DNA could not be verified, and he could not be registered. In short, this beautiful moorland pony was going to be denied his right to be called an 'Exmoor pony'. When compared to the ponies in the two pedigree herds running out on the Dunkery Commons, it was clear that Monsieur Chapeau bore a striking physical likeness to these ponies and we all felt that he had most definitely been born and bred on the moor. We were left perplexed.

The quest continues to get Monsieur Chapeau his due recognition to be called an Exmoor Pony and questions are being asked about the Exmoor pony DNA parentage verification system and whether it needs to be reformed to provide more of a 'safety net' for Moorland Exmoor ponies who are not able to be seen with their dam at weaning time. The future perhaps lies in embracing the advancement of DNA whole genome testing which will confirm whether a pony is 'pure Exmoor' or not – as it is not always possible to easily identify the parents of ponies living wild and free on the big moorland enclosures. As a result of Monsieur Chapeau's case, other identification anomalies involving Moorland Exmoor ponies have come to light and concerns are being expressed at the number of ponies being excluded from registration, and therefore lost from the breeding gene pool. Soon we would be going through the same procedure with the two moorbred yearlings, Annie Ridd and Tom Faggus and we hoped for better results.

No Exmoor Pony Showing for Monsieur Chapeau

Sadly, because he could not be registered in the Exmoor Pony Society Stud Book, Monsieur Chapeau was now not able to enter any Exmoor pony breed showing classes. This is a problem for any purebred 'Exmoor' pony whose parents can't be identified through the DNA system or those who may 'fail' the physical inspection for minor cosmetic reasons, such as a few white hairs or a pale patch on the underneath of a foot – despite otherwise being perfectly good ponies. As Monsieur Chapeau was turning out to be such a smart pony who looked like he'd enjoy going to a show and meeting people and other ponies, this was disappointing. Fortunately for Monsieur Chapeau, the recently established Moorland Exmoor Pony Breeders Group (MEPBG) had created a pioneering new show for the Exmoor Ponies of Exmoor National Park later in the summer, which welcomed both registered and unregistered Exmoor ponies. So Monsieur Chapeau would be going to a show after all!

Two True Moorland Type Exmoor ponies together – it is hard to believe that Monsieur Chapeau, on the right, may not be an Exmoor pony

Opposite: A beautiful Exmoor pony – but who is Monsieur Chapeau?

Chapter 7

Time to go Showing

Preparing for the MEPBG Exmoor Pony Show

With only a few weeks to go before the show, which was taking place in early August at the historic Brendon Show, there was much to be done to prepare Monsieur Chapeau – and the other three Moorland Exmoor yearlings we wanted to take.

Part of this included ensuring that they were confident with leading out in a head collar, loading into the trailer and, importantly, being able to cope with the hustle and bustle of a horse show. To begin, we took Monsieur Chapeau for a short walk into the woodland area, which is adjacent to the farm. He enjoyed meandering along the paths, navigating the stream and generally having a look around. However, he was soon keen to return to the security of what he now called home – the farm. Perhaps he remembered what it was like to be all alone in the forest. So while Chapeau

Opposite: Monsieur Chapeau on his first walk out in the forest with Dawn

Below left to right: Monsieur Chapeau with Dawn meeting the teleporter; Monsieur Chapeau practising agility with June Eckhart; Farleywater Lady Stumpkin Pumpkin spotting the lawnmower, with Kate South

was brave and calm in temperament, it was clear that he too would need careful preparation to find the confidence to cope with a show environment. As usual, he was our barometer.

The yearlings we'd selected to take to the MEPBG Exmoor Pony Show were all still quite wary of being closely handled and leading out in hand, as is normal for wild Exmoor ponies – and perhaps the idea of taking four yearlings all at once to their first show was a little ambitious! We'd decided to take Anchor Imperial Topaz, Monsieur Chapeau, Farleywater Lady Stumpkin Pumpkin and Farleywater Scarlet. They were still very much 'babies' and had different personalities and ways of approaching and dealing with new things. What I ideally wanted to do was organise some walks out around the lanes and fields and agility play sessions with them all together, but for that I needed some assistance. Fortunately, help was at hand with experienced horsewomen June Eckhart, Judy Bethell, Kate Hele and Kate South (whose family own the Farleywater H67 herd), who were all kind enough to visit us at Holt Ball at least once a week, or when they could manage it, and we had a series of little practice sessions with the yearlings.

Walks Out, Show Ring Training and Agility

The show preparation ranged from short walks out and about, where they could meet new things, to some agility play, and walking around a practice show ring in a field. We decorated it with some bunting which flapped in the breeze and parked the kind of objects they might see at a show around the outside. And we endeavoured to make it fun for the ponies who enjoyed their 'grazing breaks' on their trips out – munching some fresh herbage and taking in the different surroundings. We also got them used to things like flags, gates and vehicles – and the farm activities provided plenty of opportunities to meet new things – from teleporters to lawnmowers. It was fascinating to see how they responded. Monsieur Chapeau was calm and very interested in everything – especially fresh grass – but he didn't like flags at all at first. And he had his own opinion on how things should be done which could include firmly planting his feet at times. However, when I took him out for a walk on his own, he suddenly gave an astounding impression of Zebedee – leaping about all over the place! A timely reminder of the mighty spirit that lurked inside the normally composed Monsieur Chapeau. Lady Stumpkin Pumpkin was more cautious and had to be convinced that trotting was a good idea, at which point she would suddenly burst into a breathaking trot, full of impulsion – but only when she wanted to. Topaz was sensitive, responsive and keen to trot and although I'd expected him to be rather flighty, he surprised us by understanding that staying with his handler was a good idea. He was a dream to lead and keen to please. The breathtakingly beautiful filly Farleywater Scarlet was more unsure, and a little behind the others in development. She tended to want to take flight when uncertain about anything and

Opposite, clockwise from top left: Monsieur Chapeau has a good look at the lawnmower; Monsieur Chapeau on his way out for a walk with Dawn; Monsieur Chapeau and Lady Stumpkin Pumpkin doing some show training in the field with Dawn and Kate

Above: Lady Stumpkin Pumpkin and Monsieur Chapeau with Kate Hele, Kate South, Dawn Westcott and Valerie Powell

Right: The ponies teach themselves to load in the trailer

Opposite: The show team – from left, Farleywater Lady Stumpkin Pumpkin and Kate Hele, Anchor Imperial Topaz and June Eckhart, Farleywater Scarlet and Dawn Westcott and Monsieur Chapeau and Judy Bethell

managed to demonstrate this in an alarming manner on most days – even when I had her on a 20ft rope to allow for the extra 'flight response'. Yet she also delighted us by remembering her recall and the 'come to me' during the moments when she would burst away across the field with the lead rope trailing behind her. Scarlet highlighted the value of liberty foal socialisation – and that once the connection is created, the ponies will always come back to you when they get loose – which does happen with Exmoor ponies from time to time. I was pretty certain that she was going to produce this behaviour at some point during the show...

Loading Training

In order to get the ponies used to loading we parked the horse trailer in their field and opened up both the front and rear ramps. They were then free to explore to their heart's content. I wondered how long it would take them to brave the trailer as I walked across to the barn to fetch my camera. Amazingly, I heard a clunk-clunk noise almost straight away, and when I returned, there were Lady Stumpkin Pumpkin and Topaz, peering out from inside the trailer. Pumpkin took a couple of

attempts to work out that she could actually touch the front ramp when exiting the trailer and soon they were all stomping in and out, thoroughly enjoying this new agility obstacle. We then included a walk through the trailer after a training session and when we progressed to loading them in a lorry the day before the show, the ponies had no problem with the rather formidable, steep ramp. They had literally taught themselves to load. Once again, when asking the ponies to load, the 'Draw To Me' invitation worked very well as they understood what they needed to do, and trusted us. Even Scarlet was managing to temper her natural flight response and did everything along with the other ponies. She was benefiting enormously from peer group learning. With their summer coats gleaming and their confidence growing, the Show Team of Moorland Exmoor Foal Project ponies looked exciting and we were looking forward to the show.

Keeping 'A Smile in the Line'

Some 'traditional' methods of leading a pony involve keeping a tight hold of the rope right up underneath the pony's chin with an elbow pressed close into the pony's shoulder. This method of leading can be exhausting as it usually results in a tense and resistant pony, whose natural movement is restricted – and backache for the handler. We prefer to try to keep a 'Smile in the Line'. In other words, the rope is there connecting the pony and the handler, but it's not there to

Opposite, clockwise from top left: Lady Stumpkin Pumpkin takes a couple of goes to realise you can touch the ramp when exiting; Imperial Topaz is the bravest; Topaz demonstrating how ponies should load in trailers; after the liberty loading, walking through on the line is easy; Monsieur Chapeau has no problems with the lorry ramp, led by Judy Bethell

Imperial Topaz and Lady Stumpkin Pumpkin relaxed with 'a smile in the line', with Dawn and June

restrain or control the pony. Our aim is for the pony to come with us willingly, without being hauled or pulled. And if he does take fright at something, we have some clear communication tools to try to get his attention back on us and to encourage him to stay with us – that don't involve violence or discipline. We try to achieve willing participation. If a pony is relaxed and trusting of his handler, he's more likely to keep his head if he gets a fright. And if he does manage to get loose, he's more likely to come back and lower his adrenalin again soon after. So we use 12ft lead ropes made of good quality material that allow a small vibration to travel up the line when you tap them. This is another subtle way of communicating your intention to your pony, such as 'It's OK, I'm here with you – we're connected,' or 'Can you please take a step backwards.' With their sharp intelligence, ponies are extremely capable of understanding and responding to these subtle requests. Having an open, well-established connection also helps to keep them calm, especially with everything going on at a show. This is stating the obvious, but a pony walking along as a willing partner is more relaxed than a pony being led along with a hand firmly gripping the side of the bridle, with the threat of admonishment from a stick.

So all of the Show Team were becoming used to leading out with a 'smile in the line' and when the dynamics changed and the line became momentarily taut for whatever reason, they and their handlers were learning to positively communicate to restore equilibrium. As a result, the ponies were developing trust and confidence and were clearly enjoying their training. Especially Monsieur Chapeau – who by now had become fond of flags.

The MEPBG Exmoor Pony Show with Hurricane Bertha!

Finally, the day of the show arrived and it managed to coincide with the tail end of Hurricane Bertha! Rain and wind lashed down on the farm all night and we woke at the crack of dawn to a formidable gale. At 8am the show, to be held at Brendon, high up on Exmoor, was almost cancelled but the organisers decided to press ahead in true Exmoor style. Not exactly ideal conditions though, for taking four wild yearlings on their first ever showing outing. Judy and June somehow managed to sort out their own horses before arriving early in the morning along with Kate Hele – and Kate South was going to meet us at the show. After a brush and polish up, the ponies all loaded beautifully with Scarlet and Pumpkin in the trailer and Topaz and Monsieur Chapeau in the lorry – and we set off. A slight mishap occurred when the lorry malfunctioned driving up to Webber's Post and Nick telephoned ahead to Judy and myself to tell us to proceed to the show with Scarlet and Pumpkin while he swapped the lorry for the other trailer. This caused our eyes to widen somewhat at the prospect of Nick and June swapping two yearlings on their first trip in the lorry, into a trailer, half way up towards Dunkery Beacon – and we waited with some anticipation

Farleywater Scarlet with Dawn Westcott

to hear how it had gone. In the event, Nick fetched the trailer and parked the two ramps so they met when lowered and then asked the ponies to move from one vehicle to the other. Surrounding them were about 5,500 acres of open wilderness, and thankfully they did as they were asked. When you think that only a few months previously, Topaz had been completely wild and touch resistant this showed some considerable progress.

We arrived at the show ground to decidedly 'inclement' weather conditions. Monsieur Chapeau and Topaz waited in their trailer while Scarlet and Pumpkin came out to do their class. Pumpkin walked out calmly into the blustering wind and surveyed the show field. Scarlet came down the

From left to right:
Lady Stumpkin Pumpkin
with Kate South;
Lady Stumpkin Pumpkin
with June Eckhart and
judge Mr Rex Milton;
Monsieur Chapeau and
Judy Bethell with judge
Mr Rex Milton

ramp and took off with 20 ft of rope trailing behind her. She stopped about 100 yards away and decided to talk to Donna Sellick who was there with their lovely Exmoor pony Bramble. Thankfully, Donna is very quiet and gentle with the ponies and this allowed me time to approach and retrieve Scarlet. We made our way back over to the collecting area. The show was situated in a large field high up next to Brendon Common, with spectacular views across Exmoor to the sea. This allowed Hurricane Bertha the opportunity to ensure we enjoyed everything she could deliver in her powerful tail end. While the wind continued to howl around us and the rain started pelting down again, someone who shall remain nameless rushed across the field to kindly offer me a waterproof coat to put over my tweed showing jacket. Unfortunately, she also held it high above her head and Scarlet found this rather alarming, so took off again, this time right across the length of the field towards the quarry at the other end – trailing her 20ft rope. I jogged steadily after her and paused when she stopped to glance at me. Then I zig-zagged towards her, avoiding a direct approach, which could have pushed her into flight again while in this adrenalin-high state. She kept watching me. As I got within about 30 yards, I could see – and hear – a team of Clydesdale carriage horses clattering down the lane beside the field and Scarlet was near to the gate where they would shortly pass. I gestured for her to 'Draw To Me' and she responded, making her way over to me with the long rope now sodden and heavy, trailing behind her in the grass. This can cause a pony to spook as it's rather like being chased by a snake, but she remained calm and steady and I focused on keeping the connection as the carriage and horses drove by. Scarlet kept her attention on me and walked right up to me. I paused before gently taking hold of the rope and she gave a deep sigh which I reciprocated and at last, we truly understood each other. This was a joyful moment for me when I knew that we really were doing the right things with the liberty foal socialisation. She had made a willing choice to come back. We made our way back to the show ring and there lined up watching us were the two judges, steward and other farmers with broad grins across their faces. All of them knew very well the challenges of showing wild Exmoor ponies and the great camaraderie of this friendly show was already evident, despite the weather. Farleywater Scarlet and Farleywater Lady Stumpkin Pumpkin who was handled by June Eckhart, both showed beautifully and it was lovely to see these two moorland fillies, who had been born wild and free close by on Buscombe, returning to this part of the moor and so proudly representing their breed. In the class, judged by moorland farmer, Mr Rex Milton (owner of Herd 23), Lady Stumpkin Pumpkin managed to pip Scarlet to first place by producing her spectacular

The Exmoor Type Championship line-up from the left, Hawkwell Bramble with his handler Cara Whitfield-Smith, Imperial Topaz and Dawn Westcott and Monsieur Chapeau and Judy Bethell

MEPBG Exmoor Type
Champion, Anchor Imperial
Topaz and Dawn Westcott

trot at just the right moment with June, demonstrating her incredible impulsion and hock action. She went on to stand Reserve Youngstock Champion (this time handled by Kate South whose family own the Farleywater Herd H67) to the lovely three year old filly, Que Sera Sera (from the Bryant family's Herd 423) owned by Bethany Hernaman. This lovely filly eventually stood MEPBG Overall Supreme Champion of the show. While Lady Stumpkin Pumpkin had shone beyond expectations, a deep bond of trust had been established with Scarlet that morning and she made no effort to take off again that day, with either me or anyone else holding her. She was at last learning to control that electric flight instinct and trust the connection with her human handlers. The show had proved to be an enriching experience for Scarlet and for us and even though the wind was still formidable, there was no need to put them back in the trailer and they stood watching as Monsieur Chapeau and Anchor Imperial Topaz prepared for their class.

When we opened the door of the trailer, Monsieur Chapeau was lying peacefully in the straw bed taking an opportunity to have an unconcerned nap while the wind battered noisily at the trailer and Topaz looked on. They both unloaded calmly into the windy conditions and took in everything across the show ground. Both led nicely, with me leading Topaz and Judy Bethell leading Monsieur Chapeau. Nick Westcott was in charge of taking photos and Kate Hele, Sue Howes and Andrea Jones were our 'men on the ground' keeping it all together. In the Exmoor Type Youngstock class, Topaz was called in first, with Monsieur Chapeau second and another lovely little orphaned filly, Tiger Lily, owned by Hilary Williams, in third place. With three such lovely ponies in the ring it was hard for judge Rex Milton to place them. After the Exmoor Type Senior class, to our delight, Topaz went on to stand MEPBG Exmoor Type Champion. It was so good to see these lovely Moorland Exmoor ponies able to go to a show when they would normally be excluded. Monsieur Chapeau had a special red 'Monsieur Chapeau' sash which he wore proudly to greet the well-wishers who had come to see him. The ponies loaded easily again to go home. All in all, despite the weather, it was a fantastic day and we were so proud of everyone.

The Story of Que Sera Sera

The three year old filly, Que Sera Sera, who stood the Supreme Champion of the MEPBG Exmoor Pony Show, also had a very special story to tell. Her mother had sadly been hit and killed by a car crossing the Countisbury moor when Que Sera Sera was only two weeks old. That night, the foal had run away across the moor and couldn't be caught. However, the following morning, another free-living mare brought her to the farmyard and then galloped off. Her breeder, moorland farmer James Bryant, tried to get the foal to drink milk from a bottle and she refused. He kept trying but she kept refusing and as she became thinner and weaker, he resigned himself to the fact she would have to be put to sleep. He emptied the final bottle of milk into a nearby bucket and prepared to end the foal's misery. At that moment the foal walked over to the bucket and began to drink. Bethany Hernaman was working for James at the time and she took on the foal to see if she could help her to survive. The foal's strength grew and she was able to accompany Bethany and the family's ten dogs on liberty walks on the open moorland, and then follow Bethany home again. A truly special relationship was established and, like Monsieur Chapeau, Que Sera Sera (or 'Liberty' as she was nicknamed) grew into a beautiful pony. You can imagine how Bethany and her family and James Bryant felt when the filly stood Supreme Champion of the MEPBG Exmoor Pony Show as a three year old!

Que Sera Sera from Herd 423 with from left Mrs J Rawle, Mr and Mrs Hernaman and Bethany Hernaman

Chapter 8

Autumn Adventures

Monsieur Chapeau - The Equine Teacher

After the show in August, the yearling herd continued to make steady progress in their socialisation.

The four ponies we had taken to the MEPBG Exmoor Pony Show were now more advanced in their development and confidence than the others and had benefitted enormously from their outing. So our priority was to work with Tom Faggus and Farleywater Annie Ridd who had joined us back in May, as well as Farleywater Dazzler, Farleywater Firestar and our homebred Holtball Baluran – and the 2014 Holtball Herd 11 foals. Monsieur Chapeau continued to be very helpful, offering calm reassurance during the handling and play sessions and he would often graze with shyer ponies like Annie and Tom, or stand with them in the barn. In fact, Monsieur Chapeau was like a barometer and would indicate to me which ponies would benefit from some attention. A thoughtful little chap who was proving to be worth his weight in gold.

Opposite: Monsieur Chapeau greets his visitors Sue Downes and her granddaughter Amalia

Below left to right: Monsieur Chapeau and Kate Hele navigating the S-bend; the plastic hoop jump; and a ring of hula hoops

An Exmoor pony workshop
at Holt Ball

Below, left to right:
Monsieur Chapeau lies
down for visitor Fiona;
Fiona is moved that
Monsieur Chapeau lets her
sit with him; Monsieur
Chapeau adores a neck
scratch, here with Kate South

Monsieur Chapeau was also continuing to show a great aptitude for the agility obstacles and would happily navigate the See-Saw, tarpaulins, narrow gaps, drums, the S-bend, L-Bend, the plastic hoops and even crunching, noisy plastic milk containers in the Bottle Bank. Still only a yearling, the agility play was kept to relaxed, short sessions – where he could take part if he wanted to. Sometimes, I'd walk into the barn and find ponies crunching about in the Bottle Bank – and it was often Monsieur Chapeau mucking about or leading another pony through.

All of us connected to the Moorland Exmoor Foal Project have felt indebted to Monsieur Chapeau for what he's teaching us and for the joy of knowing such a wonderful, characterful pony. He has brought clarity to our belief that Moorland Exmoor ponies can make a better transition to domestic life with the right handling and experiences.

With his various visitors, the interest from the regional media, and the fact that the Moorland Exmoor Foal Project Blog had attracted over a hundred thousand views, Monsieur Chapeau was certainly helping people to connect with Exmoor ponies and become interested in the breed. Some of his visitors returned with friends and family also keen to meet Monsieur Chapeau and he would always ensure that they enjoyed a special moment and left with memories to treasure. His particular endearing party trick is to lie down and allow visitors to sit alongside him, sometimes then lying flat out while they stroke him. Anchor Imperial Topaz has also been known to remain lying down and let visitors stroke him and I wonder if he would have progressed to that level of trust without Monsieur Chapeau's help.

An Emerging Predicament for Free-living Moorland Exmoor Ponies

Alongside all of this positive progress was beginning to emerge a problem – which was the number of Moorland Exmoor ponies who were being excluded from pedigree registration despite the fact that they met the breed standard and were physically of suitable quality and type to be called an Exmoor pony. Exclusion is a serious matter because it means that the ponies – and any progeny they might produce thereafter – are forever lost from the breeding gene pool. It also excluded them from participating in Exmoor pony breed showing activities, where they could demonstrate their qualities and through that, inspire more people to become interested in the breed, who could offer ponies good homes. So the circle of opportunity for the free-living Moorland Exmoor ponies – in making the successful transition from the moor to finding good homes – appeared to have some significant obstructions for various of the ponies and their breeders.

Too many good quality True Moorland Type Exmoor ponies are being discarded

The Exmoor pony registration system is letting down ponies like Monsieur Chapeau

Above: Unfortunately, DNA testing has still not revealed the parents of Tom Faggus who is a beautiful and True to Type Exmoor pony

Left: Farleywater Annie Ridd's DNA confirmed her as being by Moorland Kingfisher out of Amethyst

Good News for Annie Ridd but not so Good for Tom Faggus

During the autumn, we received the news that Farleywater Annie Ridd's DNA test had verified her as being sired by the stallion Moorland Kingfisher (as we expected and the same as the other Farleywater foals), and out of a Farleywater mare called Amethyst (a different Amethyst to Topaz's mother). This meant that Annie Ridd could be inspected and hopefully fully registered as an Exmoor pony. However, the initial DNA test result for Tom Faggus did not reveal his sire or dam. He also bears a striking physical likeness to the Farleywater progeny by Moorland Kingfisher and as he too was gathered in from their moorland enclosure on Buscombe, the failure to identify his parents remains somewhat of a mystery. The quest continues to confirm this lovely pony as a genuine purebred Moorland Exmoor – along with Monsieur Chapeau.

Monsieur Chapeau and Tom Faggus are two glaring examples of perfectly good Moorland Exmoor ponies who, through the current system, are not able to be classified as Exmoor ponies and are therefore excluded from 'the breed'. We were also becoming aware of a number of Exmoor ponies across the moorland enclosures which were in the same predicament, sometimes including the entire annual foal progeny of various Moorland Exmoor pony herds. As the failure to secure suitable registration makes it extremely hard to sell the ponies, there is a high risk of such ponies being culled. Various of the Exmoor moorland farmers and land owners are working with the authorities to try to address these problems and work out how to improve the situation.

The Autumn Exmoor Pony Gatherings

During the autumn we were privileged to experience the gathering of the famous Tippbarlake Herd 387 from Brendon Common, a vast moorland area where the various enclosures span some 6,000 acres. It was a magnificent sight watching the largest free-living family-owned herd of Exmoor ponies in the world cantering in across this breathtakingly beautiful wilderness terrain and streaming into the home farm at Brendon Barton. This herd, owned by the Floyd family, was founded with bloodlines from Moorland Herds 1 and 10 (Bob Westcott). As I highlighted earlier, living and breeding in their indigenous natural environment helps the ponies retain their special characteristics and behaviours and the preservation of herds like this is vital for the future of the 'True Moorland Type' Exmoor pony. With their blond-tipped flowing manes, lovely movement, attractive looks and incredible hardiness – which enables them to survive and thrive in this unforgiving terrain all year round – it is easy to be in awe of these gorgeous ponies.

The Tippbarlake 2014 foals are still not DNA parentage-verified but all passed the breed inspection and met the breed standard

Finding Good Homes for Moorland Exmoor Foals

During the autumn, the adventures of Monsieur Chapeau and his siblings continued to generate interest and positive publicity through the pictures, blogs, articles and videos posted on social media and the Exmoor Pony Club website. Through this and the collaboration with and marketing efforts of our fellow Exmoor farmers, some lovely new owners were found for various of the moorland foals. This included two lucky colt foals from the Farleywater Herd who travelled all the way to Southern Bulgaria to their new home with Amelia Phillips. Some of the moorland herds managed to find homes for all of their foals. However, our hearts went out to the Tippbarlake Herd, which encountered problems with the registration and DNA parentage verification process and, after waiting months for passports, discovered that the foals were being issued with non-pedigree passports despite them passing their physical inspection and meeting the breed standard. Sales were lost through the delays and uncertainty – and it is much harder to find good homes for strapping, 'non-pedigree' wild, unhandled yearlings than it is for newly weaned foals who are less daunting to socialise. Work continues to sort out the situation.

Above: Ian and Kate South gathering the Farleywater H67 Herd

Opposite, clockwise from top: Exmoor farmer, Ian South, bringing the Farleywater H67 Herd across Brendon Common; The Molland Herd 99 ponies waiting in the pens; Tippbarlake Herd 387 coming home to Brendon Barton

Chapter 9

Winter Adventures

Monsieur Chapeau's Christmas PhotoShoot

With Christmas on the horizon, we came up with the somewhat ambitious idea of asking Monsieur Chapeau and some of the other ponies to wear tinsel garlands for a Christmas card photoshoot. And for Monsieur Chapeau to wear a tall Santa Claus hat.

Amazingly, they complied and of course, Monsieur Chapeau didn't mind at all. Festooned in a tinsel garland, he was more interested in munching the haylage. Lady Stumpkin Pumpkin was more cautious about the tinsel but after watching Monsieur Chapeau's acceptance of this strangely sparkly and shiny material, she too accepted a garland. Even Topaz wore tinsel in his forelock. Monsieur Chapeau did widen his eyes as the hat kept toppling over. But once again, he was a little trooper and the job was done. The resulting Christmas cards were a success for the Moorland Exmoor Foal Project and sold out. Monsieur Chapeau and his friends had done it again.

Opposite: Monsieur Chapeau with his tinsel garland

From left to right: Monsieur Chapeau and Lady Stumpkin Pumpkin; Imperial Topaz is happy to wear tinsel; Monsieur Chapeau manages to keep the Santa hat on long enough to get the photo

Top: The MEPBG/ AH Saddles Exmoor Type Championship Final Qualifiers

Above: Best Exmoor Pony rosettes for the qualifying ponies

The Creation of the MEPBG/ AH Saddles Exmoor Type Championship Final Qualifiers

The Exmoor farmers in the Moorland Exmoor Pony Breeders Group were concerned that various Moorland Exmoor ponies, through no fault of their own, were being excluded from pedigree registration and, as a result, were thereafter presented as rather 'second rate goods' – when in fact, many of them were good quality 'True Moorland Type' Exmoor ponies. It was clear that any changes to the system would take a long time so something had to be done to help the ponies in the meantime – both to safeguard and protect them and also to help motivate people to offer them good homes. Presenting such ponies as 'failures' or 'unknowns' made it difficult to find homes and the alternatives for the ponies were not good. With the number of female foal registrations dropping to under seventy each year, the breed cannot afford to waste suitable purebred genetics. So the farmers wanted to give these ponies some much needed recognition and opportunities. The MEPBG Exmoor Pony Show, with its 'Exmoor Type' classes and championship had been a good start and after discussing the situation with Medwin and Richard Broad of the South West Pony Association, it was decided to create a series of Qualifiers at each of their SWPA shows. Exmoor ponies who found themselves outside of pedigree registration, would compete and qualify for an 'Exmoor Type' Championship Final which would be held at the annual MEPBG Exmoor Pony Show at Brendon. The Best Exmoor entering the Hill & Moorland Pony Classes would qualify – and the five SWPA shows covered a large area, from Wales to Dartmoor, giving plenty of opportunities to take part. It was the start of positive recognition for lovely ponies like Monsieur Chapeau who would otherwise be excluded from the Exmoor pony show ring.

Monsieur Chapeau recovering from his upset tummy and joining the rest of the herd

Monsieur Chapeau gets an Upset Tummy

Over the winter Monsieur Chapeau experienced periodic bouts of what I can only describe as 'runny poo'. We were aware that, having been found in such a malnourished state as a foal with a significantly swollen belly, that he may well have some ongoing issues with his gut. Overall, he looked good and kept his condition on a high forage diet, with access to a mineral lick and salt and some occasional high fibre pony feed. But at times, he seemed to be struggling a bit and I was thinking he needed some help when it was suggested that we add a charcoal supplement to his diet. This together with a probiotic powder was added to a good quality high fibre feed. Over a period of weeks, he started to show steady and consistent improvement and supplementing his forage diet like this when necessary seems to be continuing to keep his tummy in good shape.

Pasture Management for Exmoors Living in Paddocks

When Exmoor ponies live on large moorland enclosures of hundreds and even thousands of acres, they have access to a wide range of rough vegetation and forage. They can nibble at various coarse moorland grasses, bushes, trees, roots, flora such as gorse and heather, etc, and lick minerals from the soil and rocks when they need them. Their guts are designed to deal with a continual intake of rough forage, often grazed for at least sixteen hours a day, and they have to keep walking to find it. When they're kept in paddocks, they are very much reliant on their humans to provide what they need in the way of nutrients and minerals. And if they have access to rich pasture grass without having to do much work to find it, this can result in them rapidly gaining weight – even in winter. Some people react to this by keeping their ponies in at night or during the day. However, Exmoors don't enjoy being shut in stables for long periods and they should never go without access to some kind of forage for very long as this can result in an increase in stomach acidity and lead to ulcers and colic, just like any other type of equine. So some thought and creativity is needed for pasture and stable/barn management.

Careful pasture management is important for Exmoor ponies living in-ground

Left: Creating tracks encourages the herd to keep moving and stops them gorging on too much rich grass

Tracks and Forage

One of the ways of dealing with too much grass and not enough exercise is to create areas where the ponies need to walk more to find their food and we do this by fencing off large areas in the centre of the fields – and letting the ponies walk around the outside areas. This prevents them from standing in the middle of the field gorging grass. We also feed high-fibre, dryish, meadow haylage and hay, and place it in and around the barn and corral areas, so they keep some dry forage going through their digestive system. Grass can have alarming rises in sugar at different times of the day and year (winter and summer), which can trigger conditions like laminitis. Ideally, the ponies also benefit from access to some non-grassy areas, like tracks, hard surfaces and wilder areas – including stony, rough ground, bark chips, gravel, sand, concrete, streams and pond areas, woodland, copses or even a few trees to hang around. The different surfaces help the ponies to keep their feet in good shape and healthy, as they would do out on the moor. Although creating tracks with a variety of surfaces isn't always possible, there are various improvements that can be made with a little creative thinking. Holistic natural living environments are important for their health and wellbeing. They love to play, explore, hide and hang out in covert areas and encounter things to think about and puzzle over. Watching herds of Exmoor ponies is fascinating – they are busy, inquisitive and adventurous alongside the time they spend eating, grooming and relaxing.

Certainly it was a relief when a combination of environment and some supplementary feeding, enabled Monsieur Chapeau to maintain a healthy digestive system and he shone with good health, even with his thick winter coat.

Above left: The colts and other horses in the herd can wander along interesting tracks and through and over streams

Above right: Different surfaces, including stones and rough ground help the ponies to keep their feet in good condition

Opposite: Colts Farleywater Lycan and Daemon have the benefit of a specially-created wilderness area at their home in Southern Bulgaria with Amelia Phillips

Monsieur Chapeau Goes to the SWPA Winter Woollies Show

The first MEPBG /AH Saddles Exmoor Type Championship Final qualifying show took place in January 2015 at the Stretcholt Equestrian Centre in Bridgwater, Somerset. It was well named 'The SWPA Winter Woollies Show' and Monsieur Chapeau was certainly living up to that description with a spectacular flowing winter coat and beard. His mane and tail still retained some of the flame-coloured tips from the summer and he looked great. Like every proper Exmoor pony, he'd spent the winter without a rug as their amazing double-layered, shaggy coats provide all the protection they need. Now we just had to remind Monsieur Chapeau what he needed to do in the ring, so a bit of leading practice was required. When we organised some 'ring practice', I needn't have worried and he soon got the idea again. As it was still rather cold, I decided to give MC a good groom rather than an actual bath and he polished up well with a gleaming shine. On the morning of the show he loaded with no problem and off we went.

Despite it being January, there were horses and ponies of all different shapes, sizes and colours at the show and the equestrian centre was bustling and busy. We unloaded Monsieur Chapeau in the yard and he was looking around wide-eyed when a lady marched past with a small pony who was objecting to something or other. This resulted in a loud smack and admonishment from the lady, causing the pony to spin around. Monsieur Chapeau literally leapt out of his skin and bolted towards the muck heap with me in tow. Fortunately, his flight response was short and he didn't quite deliver us into it, thankfully pulling up just before. 'It's OK Monsieur Chapeau,' I reassured him, 'the nasty lady isn't going to come and hit you.' MC stood there panting as he realised that ponies could actually be smacked!

Fortunately, this was the only time we witnessed such behaviour and Monsieur Chapeau soon got used to being surrounded by all the different equines. He whickered to them and showed a keen interest in everything, including other people's bags, grooming kits and buckets. As most of the waiting areas were on concrete, there wasn't anything for him to graze so he busied himself with watching the proceedings.

Soon it was time for the class which was taking place in the indoor arena. Although rather apprehensive at the gallery of people and new surroundings, we entered the ring and started walking around with purpose until Monsieur Chapeau spotted himself in the wall of mirrors at the far end. It took some persuasion for him to tear himself away from the rather smart pony staring back at him. Then it was time for a trot and he decided to add in some leaps and a canter to show his full range of movement. The judge fortunately found this quite amusing and on inspecting him at close quarters during his stand up commented that you 'couldn't find more of a moorland type

Monsieur Chapeau at the
SWPA Winter Woollies Show

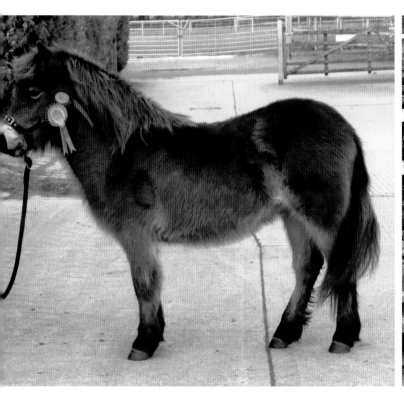

than this.' Monsieur Chapeau was awarded his rosettes and had qualified for the MEPBG/AH Saddles Exmoor Type Championship Final. Afterwards, it was time for a photocall with the rosettes attached to his head collar and then a wait outside for the In Hand Championship, where he was particularly mesmerised by the Shetlands and miniature horses. The open championship included an eclectic variety of equines and provided Monsieur Chapeau with some excellent ring experience. The steward kindly offered a click of encouragement when it was his turn to trot which resulted in an impressive 'almost handstand' before an exuberant 'go around'. We would definitely need to do a little work on 'impulsion without gymnastics' before the MEPBG Championship Final.

After such a busy day, Monsieur Chapeau was delighted to return home to his herd and strolled from the trailer into the corral with what can only be described as a swaggering gait, clearly very proud of himself. The local West Somerset Free Press entered into the spirit of things and published a picture of Monsieur Chapeau with his rosettes, giving some much needed positive publicity for the Moorland Exmoor ponies. It was a good start.

Left: Monsieur Chapeau at the SWPA Winter Woollies Show

Right: Monsieur Chapeau busy exploring other people's grooming kits

Chapter 10

The Terrible Twos and Inspections

At around the time of taking Monsieur Chapeau to the SWPA Winter Woollies Show I started to notice that he was becoming rather cheeky.

This is a normal phase in youngsters, particularly when they haven't been suppressed with punishment in their training and handling. While Monsieur Chapeau had experienced a very tough start in life, every interaction he's had with humans has been kind and friendly. As he's matured and found his confidence and place in the herd, it was only natural for him to start 'pushing the boundaries', asking questions and seeing what he could get away with.

So if, for example, he thought he needed a feed, he'd start trotting up behind me and giving me a nudge. If someone came to visit, he'd go up to say hello and give them a playful nip. And he would make it clear that if food was around, nothing was going to stop him getting to it. These are all natural behaviours and his love of food is entirely understandable given the starvation he suffered as a foal. But there are acceptable ways to behave so Monsieur Chapeau needed to learn appropriate behaviour, just like the rest of us.

How to Deal with the Testing Two Year Old?

The temptation when faced with a cheeky and sometimes quite naughty two year old pony, can be to administer instant 'discipline'. The reason (or excuse) given for delivering a sharp smack, poke, shove or other rather aggressive gesture to a questioning youngster is that the pony 'must learn to respect you or it will become spoilt.' At the other end of the scale, if people don't assert themselves at all, they can find they get nipped, barged and even kicked and subsequently become nervous of the pony. When the pony senses this apprehension it can trigger anxiety – because where there is no mutual trust, there is likely to be an increased chance of unpredictable behaviour

Opposite: Ponies experiencing Terrible Twos can go through a nipping stage

from the human. And unpredictable humans can become fearful and aggressive, which can compromise the pony's safety – and as a result, young ponies can become mistrustful and even defensive. Not dissimilar to the human equivalent – or indeed a 'teenager' struggling to find themselves. So remaining calm and confident is essential for good pony communications, especially during this questioning phase. It is also important to be clear and consistent and ensure that our responses are appropriate to the pony's behaviour. Adrenalin must be kept low (ours as well as the pony's) and we need to make it clear, in a reasonable manner, which behaviours are acceptable and which are not.

Being Clear and Consistent

Youngsters are quick to learn the wrong as well as right behaviour – and they can become annoyed and insecure if they get mixed messages from handlers. A good example is if someone walks up to a pony, wraps their arms around his neck and gives him a scratch and a cuddle which he finds pleasurable. He sees this close contact and scratching as friendly, sociable 'herd' behaviour. So when the handler is in close proximity another time and the pony moves right in and starts nuzzling and rubbing his head against the handler, that is not the time to smack him away in order

Above left: Monsieur Chapeau and Imperial Topaz demonstrating Terrible Twos

Above right: Young ponies are simply asking questions as they grow up – Monsieur Chapeau

Opposite: Young ponies can go through the Terrible Twos – Monsieur Chapeau peeking through from the back here

Dawn Westcott rewarding good behaviour – Monsieur Chapeau is lying down on the left hand side and Topaz is sniffing Dawn's hand with Dazzler and Scarlet looking on

Right: Ignoring the bad behaviour and rewarding the good behaviour works with the Terrible Twos

for him to 'respect the handler's space'. Because the pony will be very confused about what is and what isn't allowed with regard to close contact. And the trust a pony builds in a handler can start to be lost if the pony is not sure what the 'rules' are, with regard to behaviour when in close proximity to a human. Once again, remaining mindful and thoughtful about what we're trying to convey to the pony and endeavouring to see it from the pony's point of view prevents misunderstanding.

Ignore the Bad Behaviour and Reward the Good Behaviour

When a pony is going through this naturally testing time, I try to ignore the bad behaviour and reward the behaviour that I find acceptable. So while I do allow ponies to come up and explore me, I endeavour to show them through reasonable, non-aggressive body language that I don't like barging, nipping, defensive back-ends or anything to do with kicking whatsoever. When this occurs, I will look to distract them into a more appropriate behaviour rather than 'discipline' the behaviour I don't like.

The Cautionary Squeal – a Useful Tool

Sometimes, you do need to quickly stop a particular behaviour in its tracks – for reasons of safety. The 'Cautionary Squeal' is a fantastic communication tool at such times. It's most effective when applied during the earliest signs of undesirable behaviour. Take nipping, for example. A pony will normally make one or two small gestures indicating that he's shortly going to attempt to nip. So a sudden sway or move towards me, a flickering of ears, or a playful (or not) pre-nipping gesture, will cause the pony to receive a small, shrill squeal or shriek from me – then an immediate return to the calmness of what we were doing before. This may have to be repeated a number of times, but a squeal usually makes it quite clear to a pony that I don't like what he's doing or is thinking about doing. Mares and fillies, as well as stallions and geldings, often give out little squeals when conveying to other ponies that something is not acceptable – and the timing is often before the undesirable behaviour actually occurs. The trick is to be consistent and try to time the squeal so it clearly relates to the undesirable behaviour. If necessary you can also raise your energy and convey that the pony should take a step away – without appearing aggressive or making physical contact. Bringing your energy up with a demonstrative gesture is far better than administering a sharp smack or shove, which the pony will interpret as aggressive and therefore, unreasonable. Horses engage in an entire language of subtle communications before actually biting, kicking or lunging at one another – and learning to convey what you like and don't like through non-violent communications builds trust and understanding. Even if a passer-by may think you quite mad, the ponies will completely understand you.

Don't Bite the Pony Back!

Once a pony actually delivers a proper nip, it's likely that the signs leading up to it will have been missed by the handler, and by this time the pony is probably quite annoyed that he hasn't been listened to. Becoming more mindful and observant of what ponies are trying to convey and communicate greatly assists in keeping them calm and polite – and in the handler not getting nipped. Most people can get a bit agitated if they feel they're not being listened to and ponies are no different. Like us they have different personalities and moods, and respond and react to things differently – so will have various levels of tolerance in any given situation. One thing that I would never do is bite a pony back that has just nipped me. The justification for this is that 'horses do this to each other, so I'm only showing him in his own language.' I disagree – all you are doing if you bite a pony back is confirming that this kind of behaviour is acceptable to you. A disaster. While the pony may not bite you again, he will certainly not trust you either – because you've behaved like the predator he knows you are. If someone kicks a football through your window, you don't go around to their house and kick a ball through their window. You indicate to them that this was not acceptable behaviour. And so it is with ponies. Consider a nip a lesson that you have missed all of the preceding communicative signs from the ponies, and resolve to pay more attention in future.

Giving the Terrible Twos the Attention they Crave

Trying to be receptive, observant, clear, consistent and reasonable in your interactions with the pony going through the Terrible Twos can help enormously in tempering their undesirable behaviour. They are simply exploring the boundaries, asking questions, trying to understand their own place and 'power' as they grow up and are not, I believe, actually trying to be 'bad' or 'aggressive'. Grooming is a good way of negotiating better behaviour from a Terrible Two. During this stage they are generally keen for attention and can become jealous and irritable if they are not the centre of it. I deal with this by endeavouring to give the ponies equal amounts of attention, and the Terrible Two has to deal with the fact that, while he will get his attention, the other ponies deserve attention too. I look to give the pony my attention when he's being good or patient, to encourage him to continue that line of behaviour. Over a fairly short time, this rumbunctious phase passes and the youngster learns that by doing the right things, he gets the attention he craves. He learns what I like and don't like. Importantly, he is reassured that, although he may have to wait for his turn, the attention will come – and it will be positive. Ponies who don't get enough attention can become 'sulky' and jealous of their siblings. So while we might say the pony is being naughty, often we have to look to ourselves to work out the reason why. Inevitably, they are trying to communicate something. I don't believe ponies get up in the morning working out ways to be naughty, nippy, bolshy, nasty or annoying – or spoilt. But I do believe that all these behaviours can manifest themselves if the ponies feel they don't have what they need, or are confused, bored, not able to convey or express their feelings – or do not understand what is being asked of them. Respect is a mutual thing and I'm sure ponies appreciate clear communication and being treated with respect as much as humans do.

Energy Up – Adrenalin Down

One thing that is guaranteed to escalate bad behaviour with Terrible Twos is to react with raised adrenalin, aggression or forceful discipline. This simply reinforces to the pony that these kind of responses are acceptable – as you are doing them too. When you watch mares with their foals, the dams seem to have limitless depths of tolerance for cheeky foal behaviour and convey their feelings with little squeals, nudges, clear body language and pauses. And when they want the foal to do something, like move quickly away, the foal is locked on and responding without question

Opposite, clockwise from top left: Monsieur Chapeau loves attention – here with Dawn; Imperial Topaz enjoying a scratch from Judy; giving young ponies plenty of attention helps them feel confident and fulfilled; Imperial Topaz enjoying a wither scratch from June

or quibble – and understanding straight away what must be done. However, while the foal's dam will radiate extraordinary tolerance, other mares in the herd are much more forthright in their treatment of foals that are not their own, and tolerate no nonsense whatsoever. But again, they communicate very clearly, often with big gestures, and even threats – sometimes pulling the most awful faces and snaking their necks – but no actual violence, and the foal is very quick to process and understand what is being conveyed. Other communications are soft and affectionate. All this is based on body language, use of energy (not adrenalin), a series of little squeals, whickers and breathing, pauses and 'action'. And literally as soon as they have applied some of this 'pressure communication' to a foal, they return to calmly doing what they were doing before. Their energy has come up, without adrenalin, and it is brought down again very quickly. This ensures that the herd remains safe because raised adrenalin can cause irrational behaviours and is therefore dangerous. It's also interesting watching stallions teaching and playing with foals and they too can exercise incredible tolerance of cheeky behaviour and yet quickly put a foal in his place with demonstrative but non-violent communications. Foals are always in awe of and adore their fathers if they are lucky enough to spend time with them. We can learn an enormous amount about improving our own communications with ponies (and people) by watching herd interactions and trying to learn some of the subtleties and nuances of the language of horses.

Moving Through Terrible Twos Without Losing Sparkle!

The Terrible Twos can learn about acceptable behaviour without losing their confidence and sparkle through excessive discipline or negativity being applied from their handlers. Monsieur Chapeau, Pumpkin, Firestar, Topaz and all the youngsters have managed to navigate through this tricky stage and we have somehow retained our sanity and sense of humour. What has emerged are some immensely characterful and endearing ponies. And as their confidence and personalities develop, they are engaging in some amusing behaviours.

Monsieur Chapeau, for example, one day decided that it would be great fun to take the skipping-out fork out of the wheelbarrow, grasp it in his teeth and swing it about as though he was trying to clean up. It was a magical moment seeing this natural curiosity and also his intelligence in mimicking what he sees us do with the fork every day. Another regular trick is to sidle up to the wheelbarrow when it's nearly full and calmly wiggle over the handles, then pull the barrow over and watch the contents spill everywhere. It's amazing how this doesn't make the ponies spook – they just stand there looking very satisfied. If they could laugh, I'm sure you'd hear some deep chuckles ripple through the herd on such occasions. Exmoor ponies are mischievous.

Monsieur Chapeau playing with the
skipping out fork and wheelbarrow

Some Exmoors delight in dismantling jumps, where they will wiggle against and topple everything over until there's just a mass of upturned jump sides and poles on the ground – and then stand there looking smug. They will take everything out of buckets, stand in anything (I've known one to get her foot deeply embedded in a gloopy horselick), on anything, get into anything they can – and dismantle pretty much anything. The day I found five Exmoors in the feed and utility area required some considerable tidying up!

It was a great relief when Monsieur Chapeau stopped the Terrible Twos and as it happened, this was just in time for our annual Exmoor pony inspection at Holt Ball.

Inspection Time for the Ponies

Towards the end of winter, the inspection of our homebred Holtball Exmoor Pony foals (now yearlings) took place, together with Farleywater Annie Ridd and the re-inspection of Farleywater Firestar and Anchor Imperial Topaz. When the Exmoor Pony Society inspectors arrived, Monsieur Chapeau was around and about in the corral and watched the proceedings with interest. All three Holtball foals passed their inspection and Holtball Prince Kailash, Princess Karisimbi and Princess Khaleesi were now fully registered pedigree Exmoor ponies.

Then it was Farleywater Annie Ridd's turn and she fortunately passed her inspection too. It was a great relief that this beautiful yearling filly, who had evaded the autumn 2013 gathering and spent the winter out on Buscombe and Black Pitts could now be fully registered. Farleywater Firestar had been very lucky indeed. At her original inspection, she had a number of pale, greyish hairs in her mane. We had a suspicion that these may have been due to a dietary/nutritional issue of some kind and the inspectors had agreed that they would like to see her again after a coat change. During the year, the greyish hairs had naturally disappeared and of the few left, I literally only had to touch them and they fell out. A true white hair is as strong as the other darker hairs and thankfully, this was not the case with Firestar, whose proper mane was consistently dark and glossy. Other than these hairs Firestar had passed her initial inspection in every other respect. She is an absolutely beautiful pony and well-named with her bright, reddish-brown dappled coat, beautiful head and lovely dancing movement. The inspectors were satisfied and Farleywater Firestar passed her reinspection to gain full pedigree registration.

The Exmoor Pony Society rules specify 'no white markings' and this has in recent years been interpreted to include even a pale patch of pigmentation on the underneath of a pony's foot.

Opposite: Ponies won't lose their sparkle if the Terrible Twos are handled positively, allowing the ponies to retain trust in their handler. Here with Dawn Westcott

Poor Anchor Imperial Topaz remains a Section-X pony because of a small patch of pale pigmentation on the underneath of one foot despite being an outstanding pony in every other respect

Whether the pigment is dark or pale has no bearing on the quality of the foot and can be caused by simple bruising through trotting over sharp flints and stones as foals. For years, many wild foals did not have their feet picked up and no other pony breed excludes animals for the colour of the underneath of their feet. So sadly, as Anchor Imperial Topaz had a small patch of pale pigmentation on the underneath of one foot, despite being a truly stunning pony in every other respect – and as a gelding he is not a breeding animal – he could still not be fully registered and remained a 'Section-X' pony. This was a great disappointment.

What About Me? Said Monsieur Chapeau

As the inspectors walked back through the corral there, standing in front of them was Monsieur Chapeau. Of course, no one can walk past Monsieur Chapeau without saying hello and, despite his DNA parentage verification still pending, the inspectors decided to carry out his physical inspection then and there while they were on site. Monsieur Chapeau stood calmly while they looked through his mane and tail for white hairs, checked his teeth and jaw structure, took a good look at him generally and then picked up all four feet. He was completely at liberty, with no head collar on. One of the inspectors, Colin Girdler, commented afterwards that Monsieur Chapeau had 'raised the bar for behaviour at Exmoor pony inspections!' He passed his inspection with flying colours and was now deemed to have met the Exmoor pony pedigree breed standard. All that remained was for the DNA testing process to reveal who his parents were so he could be awarded pedigree status.

Chapter 11

Herd Dynamics and More Showing

Herd Dynamics

Horses and ponies have various different needs, emotions and moods – as well as characters – and these can all be influenced by the weather, hunger, health and wellbeing, herd relationships and outside influences.

So if it's windy, wet and cold and they've just had a squabble with a herd member, or if they are hungry, they might be a bit more bargy, edgy and nippy than they would be if the sun was shining on a calm day and their herd members were all mellow and happy. It's important to try to read the situation and the ponies, and gauge what connections and interactions are advisable and possible at that particular moment. The herd dynamics can also be significantly affected by the introduction of new ponies or removal of certain ponies from the herd.

Opposite: The herd dynamics change with the addition of new ponies. Here newcomer Lady Molly of Molland Moor leads Farleywater Scarlet, Imperial Topaz and Monsieur Chapeau in from the pasture

Left: Monsieur Chapeau (far right) has had a profoundly positive influence on the herd

The herd will often 'activate' and move in unison together –
here motivated by Minot the Jack Russell terrier

Top right: The ponies' behaviour can be influenced by wind, weather, time of day and hunger

Bottom right: Between bouts of playing and grazing, a well settled herd will often all lie down together too

The Introduction of Brood Mares Maisie and Georgia

The successful transition of Monsieur Chapeau's Terrible Twos had been assisted by the introduction of two older brood mares, Maisie and Georgia, into the youngstock herd while they were weaning their own foals. We like to gradually wean over a number of weeks, with the mares spending increasing periods away from the foals and then returning to them. By the time they are properly separated, both mares and foals are emotionally prepared and much happier and able to cope. Both Maisie and Georgia are strong-minded mares who take no nonsense from anyone, including a stallion, so there was no question of them taking any nonsense from a herd of two year olds, and that included Monsieur Chapeau. He learned very quickly to watch his 'Ps & Qs' and swept smartly out of the way at the flicker of an ear or a look from either of them. They commanded respect and made it clear that nothing was going to get in the way of them enjoying a particular hay pile, or moving in a particular direction. This was something of a wake up call for Monsieur Chapeau who learned not to 'look out of the Court Gate for trouble' and made every effort to ensure the attention of the mares was not directed at him. I noticed that his behaviour towards us also started to improve and with their help, we saw the return of a more thoughtful and well-mannered Monsieur Chapeau.

Below left: Brood mare Georgia lays down the ground rules to the youngsters

Below right: Monsieur Chapeau learns to exit sharply after a look from Georgia

Brood mare Maisie is also keen to establish herself

The Arrival of Lady Molly of Molland Moor

In early March, the Moorland Exmoor Pony Breeders Group (MEPBG) was involved in the gathering of the free-living herd of Exmoor ponies on Molland Moor. After many years of running wild and with ongoing problems trying to register the ponies, including issues with their DNA – the MEPBG farmers collaborated with the Molland Moor herd owner, landowner and the Exmoor National Park Authority to help gather the ponies and safeguard the future of this important moorland herd. While we were checking and inspecting the ponies, a small late-born filly caught our eye. She was no longer with her mother and yet had managed to retain her cool during the hustle and bustle coming through the pens and every time I looked across to her group, she was standing staring rather beseechingly at me. The decision was made that this dear little pony would benefit from joining the Moorland Exmoor Foal Project and she came home in the trailer with us that afternoon. Back at Holt Ball, she unloaded calmly into a large pen in the youngstock barn and met the other ponies through the gates. Her demeanour was composed and dignified and she was bestowed the grand name of Lady Molly of Molland Moor.

The Molland Herd 99 being gathered from Molland Moor with farmers James Bryant and Nick Westcott on bikes

Monsieur Chapeau took a keen interest in Lady Molly from the first moment she arrived and the next morning I found him lying down next to her pen. I watched his interaction with her and felt he would probably be the best pony to first introduce to her. When we're initiating a newcomer into what has become quite a large herd of ponies of differing ages, I try to find the pony most likely to befriend the newcomer and let them get to know one another, as we had done with Lady Stumpkin Pumpkin and Monsieur Chapeau. Then I introduce another potential friend and so on. Soon, depending on the responses of the various herd members, it's possible to let the newcomer out with the entire herd. This reduces the 'fireworks' and bullying that can occur if a new pony is just pitched into the existing herd to fend for itself.

Right: Lady Molly of Molland Moor arrives at Holt Ball

Far right: Monsieur Chapeau plays quite robustly with Lady Molly with Firestar in the background

Below: Lady Molly and Monsieur Chapeau playing

Monsieur Chapeau is Somewhat Bossy to Lady Molly!

However, when I let Monsieur Chapeau in with Lady Molly his reaction surprised me. He appeared to be rather jealous and proceeded to nudge and chase her around the barn and corral areas, nipping at her and herding her along. So Monsieur Chapeau was shooed out and Firestar came in instead. He remained keenly interested though and very quickly decided to adjust his behaviour. It was fascinating to watch him dealing with a range of emotions with regard to the newcomer. On the one hand, a little jealous of the attention she was getting, and on the other hand, he was determined to take charge of her. He was soon able to be let in with her again and he continued to lie down nearby when the herd came in and she was in her pen. After introducing various ponies to Lady Molly, including six-year-old gelding, Monty, I felt it would be safe to let her out into the pasture to interact with the whole herd. The first time was very sweet – and while the herd preferred to remain in the corral eating haylage, Lady Molly realised the field gate was open and quietly walked out with me into the pasture. She wandered a little way around the field then looked across at me and came back in. Given the choice, she preferred to be where the herd was, rather than leaving them to explore the pasture – and she showed a clear willingness to connect with me. During this interaction, Monsieur Chapeau had left the others and stood just outside the field gate watching this whole process – I felt that, once again, he was offering his help and reassurance.

When Lady Molly later went out to the pasture with the whole herd, Monsieur Chapeau was always close by, and he busily herded her this way and that. She sometimes expressed her reluctance to be guided so enthusiastically by making little bunny bucks into Monsieur Chapeau

Above, left to right:
Time for a rest with Firestar, while Monsieur Chapeau pulls faces; Monty and Lady Molly grooming; Monsieur Chapeau and Lady Molly grooming

Opposite, clockwise from top: Lady Molly tells Monsieur Chapeau to back off; Lady Molly showing her lovely paces and presence; Monsieur Chapeau herds Lady Molly; Lady Molly has an amazing turn of speed

and the odd kick in his direction. But he had very much made it his business to look after her. And that was that. Another pony who had become captivated by Lady Molly was six-year-old gelding, Monty, and he and Monsieur Chapeau took it in turns to 'take charge' of the filly, acting like guardians. Lady Molly responded by engaging in a lot of mutual grooming with Monty, which he clearly loved. She was a clever little pony and soon managed to integrate herself with the entire herd, which meant she no longer always had to be shut in the pen at night. However, she did need some extra feeds and regularly separating her from this large herd might have been somewhat of a headache, but she very soon understood that when I asked her to go into her pen, it had the positive consequence of a feed – or an opportunity to enjoy her own forage pile and a rest. She would happily leave the herd when I gestured to her, which again highlighted the benefit of establishing the 'Draw to Me' response. It was also an indication of Lady Molly's intelligence and a sign that trust was beginning to build between us.

Lady Molly Offers her Trust for Liberty Grooming

Lady Molly progressed rapidly in her socialisation and Monsieur Chapeau took a keen interest whenever I was with her. She was able to observe the other ponies being relaxed around us and allowing contact and handling. Over the preceding months the majority of the herd had become trusting, confident and engaging and Lady Molly was able to absorb and benefit from all of this. During the next few weeks, she was free to watch everything and approach us if she wanted to – and retreat when she wanted to. Sometimes, I was aware that she was standing close, just behind my shoulder and soon she would take hay out of my hand, sniff at me and give me the 'Muzzle to Hand' touch. She was intrigued when I brushed and groomed the other ponies and would watch intently. However, if I gently reached to touch her rump or make any contact at all, she would calmly and politely move away. She was interested but not yet ready to accept being touched.

As her thick winter coat started to lift and show signs of shedding I could see that Lady Molly was feeling rather itchy. So one afternoon, I again reached out gently to stroke her rump. She walked around away from me in her usual slow circle and then I asked again. This time she let me stroke her and stayed standing there. So I got out the hair brush and started gently brushing the loosening hair out of her coat. She made no effort to step away. This progressed to brushing her side and back, wither and neck. I took it very gently, aware that wild ponies can be flighty and jumpy and can suddenly decide to 'leave'. But she stayed put and started to sway and push into the brush indicating that this was feeling really good – and let me brush her on both sides. During this interaction, Monsieur Chapeau had been right next to us, doing his wonderful relaxed 'zoning in' to the session, which I had come to value enormously.

After this, Lady Molly became progressively more comfortable with being touched and would present herself for grooming, often accompanied by Monsieur Chapeau. Once she'd made the decision to allow me to touch her, she let me brush her legs, touch her feet and happily expressed her pleasure at being brushed. She would also come up in the field and showed the same affectionate willingness for interactions as Monsieur Chapeau – and I felt he had played a definite part in her progression. Even more special, was that shortly after allowing me to touch her, she allowed other people to stroke and brush her too and very quickly became very sociable and comfortable around all of us.

The Arrival of Lady Myrtleberry of Countisbury

About six weeks after Lady Molly had arrived, there was another newcomer. A tiny, late born foal (now technically a yearling) from the Bryant family's moorland Herd 423 at Countisbury, near Lynton, joined the Moorland Exmoor Foal Project. She had not over-wintered very well so seemed a little under-developed. However, she had been sired by a free-living stallion who is now in his teens and has no registered progeny, so it was thought important to safeguard this filly – and we named her Lady Myrtleberry of Countisbury after the ancient Countisbury hillfort.

Lady Myrtleberry of Countisbury arrives at Holt Ball

Her arrival coincided with the delivery of the new pony handling pen system, which had been kindly funded by the Exmoor Moorland Landscape Partnership (Exmoor National Park Authority) as part of the ongoing work to improve the pony handling facilities on Exmoor. Earlier that day, we had unloaded Lady Myrtleberry into the same gated area that Lady Molly had occupied when she'd first arrived. The delivery of the new pen system meant we had to dismantle Lady Myrtleberry's existing pen so Nick drove the bright yellow teleporter carrying the pen panels into the barn and we set about quietly removing the gates that made up Lady Myrtleberry's pen. She was then free to explore the whole barn area and she was amazingly calm for a foal straight off the moor, even walking up to sniff the teleporter and panels. We used the new panels and gates to create a 'three-room' pen area, which could be used for helping to socialise and handle the ponies. When we finished, I opened the pen door and Lady Myrtleberry walked willingly into her new accommodations. Not long after that she lay down and fell asleep – it had been a very full and busy day for her.

The new pen system proved to be outstanding for socialising Lady Myrtleberry with the herd as the ponies could line up along the whole length and Lady Myrtleberry could sniff at and get to know them all without any bullying or crowding. Lady Molly showed a keen interest in the new filly and, of course, Monsieur Chapeau was also at the front of the queue.

Top left: Lady Myrtleberry explores the new pony handling pen panels

Below: Lady Myrtleberry relaxing on her first day in the new pens

Opposite, clockwise from top left: Lady Myrtleberry meets Lady Molly; Lady Myrtleberry and Lady Molly are soon firm friends; Lady Molly protects Lady Myrtleberry as she joins the herd in the pasture; only three days after arriving, Lady Myrtleberry allows me to groom her at liberty (pictured here with yearling Holtball Princess Khaleesi)

What a Difference Three Days Make!

Socialisation was remarkably fast this time and within three days, Lady Myrtleberry was running with the herd and also allowing me to brush her at liberty. This time, Monsieur Chapeau, although rather bossy again, did not display the signs of jealously that we'd seen with Lady Molly. He seemed to be settling into his role as 'Uncle', just like Uncle Harry had been to him. He was affectionate and also chastising when necessary, and busied himself with guiding the youngsters. Lady Molly and Lady Myrtleberry became inseparable from the moment they met, and there is no doubt that the socialisation was vastly accelerated because of this. In a very short time, both Lady Molly and Lady Myrtleberry have allowed other people to groom and stroke them and we are seeing enormous benefits from facilitating peer group learning within the youngstock herd.

Introduction of the Holtball Homebred Yearlings – Changing the Herd Dynamics Again

Around the time of introducing Lady Myrtleberry, there was another change in herd dynamics as the two brood mares, Maisie and Georgia moved into another field to join two of Georgia's older

Opposite, clockwise from top: The herd relaxes in the sunshine after some gregarious play in the pasture; the ponies enjoy a group grooming session with Kate South and Lady Myrtleberry (standing centre) is settling in well; Lady Myrtleberry and Lady Molly are fast asleep with Farleywater Dazzler, while Imperial Topaz looks on

Below: The three Holtball yearlings join the herd and settle in well

Lady Myrtleberry soon befriends and relaxes with yearlings Holtball Prince Kailash and Princess Khaleesi

daughters, accompanied by Monty. Then the three Holtball homebred yearlings, Holtball Prince Kailash, Princess Karisimbi and Princess Khaleesi, were introduced into the large youngstock herd. Some of the two year olds were keen to accept and nurture the yearlings while others were more aloof. Very soon, they had all found their place and become integrated in the herd. When ponies are happy and secure in their environment and in their herd – the level of playing increases. They spent a lot of time joyfully playing followed by periods of rest. I'd often find the entire herd lying down together in the barn 'taking five' – many of them flat out asleep. Throughout these interactions, Lady Molly and Lady Myrtleberry were very much a close knit pair and moved in unison – grazing together, playing together and lying down to rest together. It was interesting to see how they were often surrounded by the older ponies when they slept, as if forming a protective ring around the youngest members. There is no doubt in my mind that being part of a happy, secure herd helps wild moorland newcomers to learn the ropes and make the successful transition to life off the moors.

Anchor Imperial Topaz Prepares to go Showing

Throughout all these activities, the previously touch-resistant Imperial Topaz had continued to be a warm, affectionate and engaging young pony – confident with both people and other ponies. We decided to take him to the next SWPA show, this time at Taunton Racecourse in early May to see if we could qualify him for the MEPBG/ AH Saddles Exmoor Type Championship Final. For a few days beforehand, I took him out for a short walk each day to ensure he was comfortable leading out and meeting several different situations. Monsieur Chapeau accompanied us on a couple of walks and one day, I asked him to trot up the long driveway and he produced the most beautiful, willing trot – with no leaps. There was hope yet. We thought about taking Monsieur Chapeau to the show as well, for some extra experience. However, his winter coat was in its most scruffy changing stage and he looked in anything but show condition. Topaz on the other hand had shed most of his coat and with a good groom and a wash through his mane and tail looked rather smart. The day before the show, we practised loading in the trailer and Topaz happily walked up the ramp so I was confident we were as prepared as we could be.

Topaz at the SWPA Trinity Show

The weather produced typical spring showers for the show – one minute dry and the next drenching everything. So Topaz stayed in the trailer and we stayed in the vehicle for as long as possible. On unloading, he took in his surroundings and soon settled. Finding and encouraging people whose Exmoor ponies have been excluded from registration is not easy, as they have thus far been excluded from the show ring. So although there were plenty of equines at the show, no other unregistered or non-pedigree Hill & Moorland ponies turned up for our class – including Dartmoors. This meant that Topaz would qualify for the MEPBG Championship Final, which was great, but we would have very much liked to have seen more ponies there. It was going to take time for people to realise that their hitherto unregistered and Section-X registered ponies were now welcome in the show ring, but at least the positive change had started.

So I used the opportunity to give Topaz some much needed show ring experience and with three busy adjacent rings the class provided more than enough activity for a previously wild two year old. He was happy to walk around and produced a lovely trot without any high jinks (Monsieur Chapeau could have done with watching this). However, something that young ponies can have trouble with is their individual trot-up. This involves walking away from the judge, then turning around at the end (as if walking around a large 'keyhole') and then a trot back towards the judge to show off their movement. For a young pony, walking away from the judge is a relief, but trotting back towards the judge is more daunting for them. I never force a young pony to do this as, in time, they will get the idea and the most vital quality you can protect in a showing pony is their 'sparkle'. That sparkle can be lost if the handler disciplines them when they are feeling uncertain. You can sometimes see a pony being pulled along or smacked to 'get it to trot'. I no longer carry a stick in the ring and try to keep a 'smile in the line' so the pony moves freely with me. As I asked Topaz to trot back towards the judge, he hesitated. I asked again and he walked forwards but he was uncertain about trotting. So we walked and I apologised to the judge and explained he was still learning the ropes, which she accepted and Topaz was awarded his rosettes.

Left to right: Anchor Imperial Topaz with Dawn Westcott with his rosettes; Imperial Topaz standing up beautifully at the SWPA Trinity Show; a relaxed Topaz taking it all in his stride

We then had quite a wait in the collecting area for the In Hand Championship and during this time, Topaz got to meet people, graze the luscious racecourse grass and watch everything going on – with ridden and in hand classes and people warming up all around him. This was fantastic experience and he remained calm and interested. When we returned into the ring for the championship, this time with a good number of other horses and ponies, Topaz kept his head and behaved very well – and offered a lovely trot. We returned to the trailer where he loaded without a problem, standing quietly inside munching his haylage while we chatted to people. The most important aspect of showing youngstock for me is that they have a positive experience. Because next time they will have a better idea of what's expected of them. Rosettes are a bonus and I was thrilled that Topaz had now qualified for the MEPBG/ AH Saddles Exmoor Type Championship Final, along with Monsieur Chapeau. But the greatest gift that day was when we returned home with a relaxed, happy pony who proudly greeted the other ponies with a satisfied sigh before ambling out into the pasture to tell them all about it. Not once during the show had Topaz tried to pull away from me or panicked – and it highlighted the value of taking the time it takes in their initial socialisation to build trust and confidence.

Monsieur Chapeau

Monsieur Chapeau continues to be a wise, generous and affectionate Exmoor pony. He is always the first, along with Topaz, Lady Stumpkin Pumpkin and Lady Molly, to raise his head in greeting across the pasture. He always comes over to say hello. When we're working with other ponies, he is interested and willing to offer his supportive and encouraging presence. It is so endearing to see him leading a youngster through the crunching plastic containers in the bottle bank, unprompted and of his own free will, or show them there is nothing to fear from the tarpaulin. If a youngster is in a pen and you walk in to find the entire herd in the adjacent area keeping them company, it is inevitably Monsieur Chapeau who is lying down closest to them. And not only does Monsieur Chapeau allow you to sit with him while he's lying down, he is also teaching the other ponies to do the same. Lady Molly of Molland Moor, and increasingly, Lady Myrtleberry, are like little carbon copies of Monsieur Chapeau – who has played such an important role in their socialisation. And of course, Monsieur Chapeau himself is looked after by Lady Stumpkin Pumpkin with whom he remains strongly connected.

What are apparent, watching this amazing herd of Moorland Exmoor pony youngsters grow, develop and flourish, are their joyful, gregarious natures, camaraderie and love of companionship and playing. Without fear and force in their training, and able to live together as a sociable herd in a natural management system, these Exmoor ponies are characterful, engaging, curious, playful,

cheeky and also thoughtful and careful. The way the ponies have embraced Lady Molly and Lady Myrtleberry is incredible. These two young fillies have so quickly become socialised to human contact and are genuinely happy in their new surroundings, which is testament to the powerful, positive energy emanating within the herd. And above all, the majority of the ponies seem to like humans and be interested and willing to engage with us. A couple of them remain shy and wary but I know it is only more time that is needed, and then they too will find their confidence in us. Central to all this is the amazing Monsieur Chapeau.

Once a starving little, late-born, orphaned Moorland Exmoor pony foal, Monsieur Chapeau now has a marvellous role in showing us how to best work with wild Exmoor ponies to win their trust and friendship. He has also helped to highlight the plight facing the free-living ponies of Exmoor National Park which has seen the Exmoor farmers and authorities coming together to work to improve the situation. We take our hats off to Monsieur Chapeau! Whether or not his parents are identified, this moorland Exmoor pony has delivered the gift of wild pony whispering with aplomb.

Above: A happy and playful Exmoor Pony herd

Opposite, top to bottom: Monsieur Chapeau with Dawn Westcott; Monsieur Chapeau watching over Lady Molly as she sleeps; Farleywater Firestar, Monsieur Chapeau and Farleywater Lady Stumpkin Pumpkin

Chapter 12
The Future for Exmoor Ponies

Although there are Exmoor ponies in various locations in the UK and overseas, their indigenous home is Exmoor National Park and the free-living herds here allow the ponies to retain the True Moorland Type.

They are able to live in genuine family herds, largely independently of man, with stallions often running with the mares and playing a role in the upbringing of foals. With such a small number of ponies, the healthy preservation and conservation of this core population of Exmoor ponies is vital for their future survival as an authentic breed.

While the moorland farmers of Exmoor are passionate about their Exmoor ponies, it should be remembered that the herds are usually maintained at considerable cost, for reasons of tradition and heritage, rather than providing a source of farming income. So it is important that the registration system for the ponies supports and encourages them in their quest to ensure that Exmoor ponies continue to live wild and free on the moors and are properly safeguarded. A system which excludes and discards good quality, true to type, moorbred Exmoor ponies like Monsieur Chapeau and Tom Faggus and many others is potentially letting down both the ponies and the herd owners.

Moorland pony management is a formidable task. In the larger, wilderness moorland areas, the various pony herds run in interlocking enclosures with multiple stallions. Sometimes, gates are left open and gaps appear in hedges and boundaries and ponies get mixed up, with stallions traversing the moorland enclosures in search of mares. In the autumn, when the ponies are rounded-up, some particularly savvy ponies are clever enough to stay out of sight – like Tom Faggus and Annie Ridd. One beautiful stallion remained ungathered for three years through his ability to stay

The free-living Porlock 100 Herd with moorland stallion Farleywater Zeus

hidden. He is now licenced and running with a different herd in another area of the moor – so we must remember that sometimes, this wilderness can produce some of the best stock through natural selection and survival of the fittest (and cleverest)! Suitable registration is needed so these amazing purebred ponies can remain part of the breeding gene pool. They are the very essence of the true Moorland Exmoor pony.

Under the current system, if DNA testing doesn't identify the parents, then neither the foals in question nor any of their subsequent progeny can be registered as an Exmoor pony. This is a source of distress for the moorland farmers who on the one hand are providing these Exmoor ponies with a wonderful wilderness environment in which to live and flourish, but who can then find themselves with 'unregisterable' ponies who are difficult to find homes for, or continue to breed from, no matter how good they are. Monsieur Chapeau and Tom Faggus were fortunate to find us, but many ponies are not so lucky.

The Exmoor farmers realise it is very important to try to ensure that their treasured ponies are appropriately recognised, and to endeavour to find opportunities and good homes for those leaving the moor. They are being strongly advised by experts and geneticists to embrace and include all possible suitable purebred genetics within the breed. Although it is not possible to bring 'additional genetics' into the Exmoor pony breed or to 'widen the gene pool' without cross-breeding (the stud book is closed), the various unregistered purebred ponies living and breeding in their moorland areas contain 'genetic variation through environment' which makes them different (even slightly) from similar bloodlines which may be represented elsewhere. These Moorland Exmoor ponies are therefore invaluable to the gene pool. When the ponies live and breed away from the moors, they start to change and over generations, there is genetic drift. We are already seeing a different 'type' of Exmoor pony evolving away from the moors. While all Exmoor ponies, wherever they live, are important and valued, more work is needed to safeguard the future of the free-living ponies of Exmoor National Park and to ensure we are recognising and embracing all possible suitable purebred genetics and upgrading their progeny wherever possible back into the pedigree breeding gene pool. The work to recognise and embrace these ponies continues and every new person who takes an interest in Exmoor ponies is helping to ensure that these majestic creatures continue to live wild and free amid the breathtaking landscape of Exmoor National Park – that landscape would not be the same without them.

With patient, positive, trust-based handling and training, Exmoor ponies can make the most wonderful family and performance ponies and turn their hooves to almost anything – including riding, driving, jumping, agility, endurance and conservation grazing. Ponies like Monsieur Chapeau

Moorland Exmoor youngsters from various different herds are being offered a good start in life with the Moorland Exmoor Foal Project at Holt Ball

Improved wild pony handling and positive, trust-based socialisation methods help previously free-living Exmoor ponies adjust to life off the moors without undue stress and trauma

are helping us to improve our horsemanship skills to get the best from them. The wild ponies of Exmoor, with their high intelligence, feisty characters and independent thinking are in a unique position to inspire horse people across the world to better understand and appreciate the amazing equine mind – and apply that to other horse and pony breeds. Orphaned Moorland Exmoor pony Monsieur Chapeau and the other Exmoors are proving to be invaluable guides in the art of wild pony whispering and are showing us the way forward.

You can find out more about Exmoor ponies and the people and projects dedicated to preserving, conserving and promoting them at www.ExmoorPonyClub.co.uk